Dedication

To all the past and present car owners who had the foresight not to restore their original cars but to treasure and preserve them as the automotive artifacts that they truly are.

It's Only Original Once

UNRESTORED CLASSIC CARS

WORDS AND PHOTOGRAPHY BY
RICHARD LENTINELLO

motorbooks

First published in 2008 by MBI Publishing Company and Motorbooks, an imprint of MBI Publishing Company, 400 First Avenue North, Suite 300, Minneapolis, MN 55401 USA

Motorbooks titles are also available at discounts in bulk quantity for industrial or sales-promotional use. For details write to Special Sales Manager at MBI Publishing Company, 400 First Avenue North, Suite 300, Minneapolis, MN 55401 USA.

To find out more about our books, join us online at www.motorbooks.com.

ISBN-13: 978-0-7603-3264-1

Editor: Peter Schletty
Designer: Claire McMaster

Library of Congress Cataloging-in-Publication Data

Lentinello, Richard A.
  It's only original once : unrestored classic cars / Richard Lentinello.
     p. cm.
  ISBN 978-0-7603-3264-1 (hb w/ jkt)
  1. Antique and classic cars. 2. Automobiles--Collectors and collecting. I. Title.
  TL7.A1L46 2008
  629.222075--dc22
                                        2008023268

Printed in Hong Kong

Contents

Introduction

Preservation Principles

Faded paint, worn upholstery, delaminated glass, and pitted chrome. These are just some of the many desirable attributes of original automobiles. Because of their irreplaceable originality, unrestored collector cars are fast becoming the single most preferred type of car that enthusiasts, collectors, dealers, auction houses, and museums want to possess.

Original collector cars should be considered nothing less than highly prized automotive artifacts. They are important transportation objects of great historical significance and provide a look back into the world of automobile manufacturing from years past.

While it's remarkable for cars built during the late 1940s and 1950s to have survived without being trashed or restored, imagine just how special it must be for cars that were produced in the 1930s, 1920s, and 1910s to retain today everything that they were first assembled with all those decades ago; or family cars to have survived unscathed after years of abuse by rambunctious children. Even more amazing are the cars of the muscle era that have remained in top-notch shape after participating in street wars and drag strip competitions.

Original cars such as these are our only glimpse into the past, thus affording us the wonderful opportunity to study firsthand the way manufacturing techniques were carried out during all of the different decades and periods of automobile production. We can see how the assembly-line workers applied the paint and inspection marks; how the upholstery was stitched and carpet was bound; how wood was cut, shaped, and joined; and which types of fasteners were used for specific applications. The same is applicable to all of a car's mechanical parts, including engine, transmission, differential, suspension, and electrical systems. Better than shop manuals, unrestored cars are existing proof to the way automobiles used to be built; they are the only true guidebook that restorers can use to ensure that the cars they are restoring are rebuilt in the most accurate, factory-correct manner.

Original automobiles such as these should be cherished. If a painting by Monet or a stained-glass panel by Tiffany shows its age, those precious works of art aren't repainted or releaded. They're lightly cleaned and left to show their age. So why then should well-preserved old cars be repainted if their original finish is still in respectable condition? After all, once that factory-applied paint is removed and the car is repainted, that car can no longer be called an original collector car. Refurbished, yes. But certainly not an original.

As more and more old cars and trucks are refurbished or restored, the survival rate of original, factory-built vehicles decreases. This means that

with each passing year there are fewer and fewer original automobiles left for the world to enjoy, appreciate, and learn from. The consequence of this trend has not only increased unrestored cars' desirability and popularity—their values have risen as well. These days, it's not uncommon for savvy collectors to pay far more for an imperfect original car than for one that's been perfectly restored.

In fact, survivor-type automobiles are now the highlight of collector-car auctions throughout the world. They have realized their own Preservation class at many of the prestigious concours competitions such as Pebble Beach, Meadow Brook, and Amelia Island. They are the center of attention at both Bloomington Gold and the Mopar Nationals. And with increasing regularity, they are fast becoming the main feature subjects upon which magazines are being sold at the newsstands.

So the next time you attend Hershey, scan the ads in *Hemmings Motor News*, flip through the pages of your local classifieds, drop in at the Lions Club car show, view an online listing, or see one profiled for sale in an auction catalog. Even if you have no plans to buy that all-original collector vehicle, take the opportunity to inspect it carefully and photograph its many factory-assembled details for future reference. This information is essential to aid restorers and car owners and ensure that all future restoration and preservation work is accomplished in the most accurate manner. The vitality and, most importantly, the respectability of our hobby depend on it.

Chapter 1

Prewar Pair: Patina Perfection of Two Great Oldies

While it is still somewhat easy to find original cars from the 1960s and 1970s, and even the 1950s, the real stars are those automobiles produced prior to World War II. With the youngest of them being nearly 70 years old, for a car to have survived more than a half century and still retain its original paint, interior, engine, instruments, and most of its mechanical components is a testament not only to the manufacturer's engineering methods and build quality but to all the previous owners who treated it with care, provided steadfast maintenance, and worked hard to preserve its originality with great respect.

But unlike survivors from the 1950s and 1960s, what is so remarkable about prewar originals is how their materials have endured for so long, materials that are far more fragile than those used on postwar cars. For instance, instead of steel-stamped wheels, cars produced prior to the mid-1930s had wheels made from separate pieces of wood. And not only did these wood-spoke wheels survive being soaked with water regularly—including summer after summer of humid weather—they also survived endless merciless pounding from rolling on rough roads, most of which were unpaved in their day.

Instead of being fitted with large bumpers to protect their protruding grille-covered radiators, many early cars had open-faced radiator cores that were extremely vulnerable to damage from road debris. For these to survive decade after decade of use and still maintain their shape and functionality is simply extraordinary. The same goes for the windshields and side glass of these cars. Unlike the fitting of laminated glass on later cars, most prewar cars had an early form of safety glass that was far more susceptible to damage. While you may notice that many windshields on prewar cars show a distinct delamination trait—

Prewar collector cars like this incredibly original 1937 Packard are still turning up in garages and barns throughout the world. This untouched beauty was sleeping in a one-car garage in Brooklyn, New York, for decades.

especially in their furthermost corners—to have lasted all these years without being cracked by an errant stone or pebble is also a significant characteristic. Also noteworthy are original glass head-lamps and taillamp lenses that survived the rigors of the road.

The most extraordinary survival characteristic of any prewar automobile has got to be the body finish. Compared to today's highly durable urethane enamels and basecoat/clearcoat urethane systems, cars from this period were painted with nitrocellulose lacquer, which was a very delicate paint finish. Lacquer is extremely brittle, and unless it is cleaned and polished regularly, it slowly loses its shine over time. And the more it's polished to retain that shine, the thinner and thinner the paint becomes. This is why, on most prewar cars (especially those of the brass and nickel eras) if they have never been repainted, you will see traces of the primer below the top coat showing through. This mostly occurs along the top of each fender and along the edges of the hood. But don't look at these cars as derelicts or being uncared for. Instead, think of them as rare time capsules of Detroit's past manufacturing techniques.

The two cars featured in this chapter represent the very best of their genre, while the prewar beauties showcased in the next chapter on Pebble Beach demonstrate the level of uniqueness that is the hallmark of this world-famous concours.

Unrivaled Roadster

A Pennsylvania original, this 1930 Oakland is appreciated for what it is, not how it looks.

I CAME UPON THIS INCREDIBLY ORIGINAL Oakland at the first All-GM Nationals at Carlisle back in June 1999. Parked on the open show field among many finely restored Pontiacs, it stood out like a Maserati parked among a lot full of minivans. It had a crowd of admirers surrounding it throughout the weekend for obvious reasons. Its paint was faded, upholstery worn, glass delaminated, and chrome pitted. Yet the most remarkable aspect of this rarely seen V8-powered Oakland roadster was that everything on it was 100 percent original, just as the Oakland factory workers assembled it all those years ago. Unquestionably, it's one of the most original, factory-correct prewar automobiles I've ever seen.

Viewing the lightly rusted paint and slightly tattered upholstery certainly doesn't distract from the car's magical appeal. Not one bit. Sure, it's not the best-preserved prewar car in existence, nor is it the most desirable, but this Oakland radiates character unlike most other original automobiles I've seen. Besides wearing its factory-applied paint and handmade upholstery, some of its many other original attributes include the convertible top, interior door panels complete with intact door pockets, radiator shell, wood wheels and center hubcaps, and the rumble seat's original upholstery, albeit weathered with a welcoming patina.

Residing in northeastern Pennsylvania, this 1930 Oakland has traveled close to 60,000 miles since it rolled off a Detroit assembly line nearly 80 years ago. Its owner, Wayne Koffel, bought it in 2000 for $25,000 from a friend and fellow Oakland club member. Because its flathead V8 had overheated, Wayne rebuilt the engine for him, at which time his friend decided to sell it. According to Wayne: "Two weeks later, I took it to the All-GM Nationals at Carlisle and two people came up to me. One was from Mecum. He made me a standing offer of $35,000 and said it was the greatest thing he'd ever seen. Next, there were two guys who owned a Pontiac dealership. They told me to name my price, and they'd write me a check."

"As far as the car goes . . . I would love to have it painted and look like it's been restored," Wayne explained. "I understand that when most people look at it, the first thing they see is that the paint is not new, they see some light surface rust, they see that it's not in concours condition. But the first thing I see, and that I saw when I decided I was going to buy it, is, 'Wow, here's a

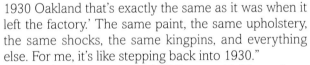

The very simple metal dash employs all its original instruments as well as its factory finish. During the nearly 80 years of passengers climbing into the rumble seat, which is still covered in the original material, the right-rear fender surrounding the aluminum step-plate proves that many of them were quite careless. At least the original grille survived unscathed.

1930 Oakland that's exactly the same as it was when it left the factory.' The same paint, the same upholstery, the same shocks, the same kingpins, and everything else. For me, it's like stepping back into 1930."

"We take trips every week," Wayne said. "Sometimes to the Dairy Queen, sometimes to dinner, but on Saturday or Sunday we'll go 100 miles or more. It handles easily; steers a lot better than a '29 model. It leans like any antique car would in the corners, but it moves. It's easy at 45 or 50 miles per hour. I had it out on Interstate 80 one time for a short distance and had it up to 70 miles per hour. With the 180-degree crank, it starts to vibrate around 45 miles per hour. The best way to describe it is, it's like a front-end shimmy without the shimmy, but when you get over 50 miles per hour, it goes away. Because of the crank, it has a really unique sound; I don't know just how to describe it."

When Wayne finds the time he tries to take it to as many car shows as work allows. "I finally took it over to Belvidere, New Jersey, where there were 120 cars at this show, all restored. My car drew the biggest crowd. I had people with restored cars come up and say, 'I wish I had a car like this.' I was amazed."

While most convertible tops hardly ever last more than 20 years, this top, installed by the Oakland factory when this car was originally assembled, has withstood the test of time beyond anyone's expectations. And regardless of its age and fragility, it still gets put down when the weather's nice.

Still powered by its original engine, this 251-ci V8 has been rebuilt to take advantage of all of its 85 horsepower. The very rare optional cabin heater, seen here on the passenger side, still blows warm air.

In desperate need of varnish, all four wood wheels and center hubcaps are original to this Oakland. And this spare tire lock, rarely seen even back in the 1930s, was installed when the car was new, and it still locks!

Hidden Treasure

Locked away in a New York City garage, this 1937 Packard existed for decades without being detected.

Brooklyn, new york, just like most old cities in the northeast, is filled with tightly knit neighborhoods with houses that were originally constructed back when the Model T ruled the road. The houses were built close together, with small one-car garages way at the back of the property. It was one of these single-car garages that housed this Packard for more than 40 years.

The current owners, Ed Memi and his son Paul, lived just a few houses away from this Packard and knew that it had been parked there since the early 1960s. Coincidentally, this Packard's garage was located directly around the block from where I lived. Sitting on the stoop of my house, I looked at the back of this garage every day during the 20 years that I lived on 22nd Street and had absolutely no idea that such a classic was hidden away inside.

Ed, who always had old cars parked in his driveway, including Model A Fords and 1930s-era Cadillacs, had

been trying to buy this car for 36 years. Paul said, "We first saw the Packard way back in 1968, then again in 1973. We tried hard to purchase it several times but it wasn't until the husband and wife who owned it were both deceased that it came up for sale." It would be another four years before Ed and Paul were allowed to view the car again; all this time it just sat there, collecting dust. Last registered back in 1963, and last used in 1964, this elegant 1937 Packard Model 1502 four-door sedan sat for a long 40 years. The original New York State Inspection stickers from 1958 and 1963 are still on the window.

When the Memis were finally able to buy the car in 2004, the odometer showed that it had only been driven 40,000 miles. No work or restoration had ever been done to this car. It's as original as the day it rolled out of the Packard factory. "All the paint, chrome, and pinstriping are intact, including the striping on the wheels," Paul said. "I used a paint gauge on the body and there are no Bondo repairs anywhere. There's no rust or wood rot present, and the car came with two original Basco key sets that fit the door, ignition, side mounts, and trunk.

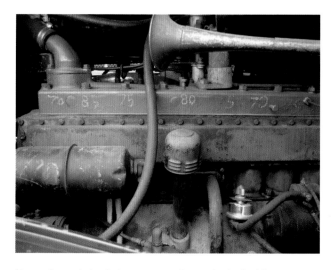

Even the original shop manual was included."

According to Paul, "Our main goal when we finally got the car was to get it running and start driving it again. First we removed the gas tank in order to thoroughly clean out all the rust particles and replace the filler neck hose. While we were working on the fuel system, we rebuilt the two-barrel Stromberg carburetor and fuel pump with the proper rebuild kits. Then we dropped the oil pan to wipe it clean of all the sludge that had accumulated in it through the years and to check the bearings, which were found to be okay. The original radiator showed no signs of leaks, so all we did was flush it out and refill it with fresh antifreeze; we also put on new hoses and had to repair the shutter thermostat. And from the head pipe back to the muffler, a new exhaust system was put in place.

"Because several valves were stuck, we had to take off the cylinder head; we then had it milled to ensure it was perfectly flat. With a new head gasket in place, and the engine filled with clean oil, we turned on the ignition and she started after just a few turns. Once the oil got hot, the oil pressure held between 20–25 psi."

Overall, the Packard survived quite well for sitting, unused for more than four decades. Besides the stuck valves, the biggest problem was the brakes. Paul and his father had to rebuild all four wheel cylinders and the master cylinder. The existing brake linings were in good condition, so they were cleaned and put back. All-new DOT 5 silicone brake fluid was used instead of conventional fluid. Once the wheel bearings were repacked with clean grease, a set of new 7.50-16 Firestone wide whitewall tires were installed along with four new inner tubes and balanced as needed.

"There were no noises coming from the 320-ci straight-eight flathead engine or drivetrain," Paul said about the Packard's first drive in 41 years. "And with new gear oil in the transmission, it didn't pop out of gear. But the

Practically every component on the straight-eight engine is not only original to the car, but still works well. The yellow numbers on the side of the cylinder head are the compression-number readings that Paul got after giving each cylinder a compression test. The original Stromberg carburetor was rebuilt prior to starting the engine once it came out of hibernation. An old Zerex antifreeze tag still hangs from where a mechanic tied it years ago.

speedometer seized while driving, causing the speedometer cable to break. As of this time the windshield wipers still do not work, nor do the clock and radio."

Some of the rarer, more sought-after parts for these prewar Packards, which this extraordinarily original example fortunately still wears, include the Goddess of Speed hood ornament, the Packard radio, the outside mirrors, and both side-mount covers. The interior upholstery is in near-perfect condition; in fact, the rear seats look as if they have never been sat upon. All the interior trim and the mohair headliner are in fine shape as well, as are the steering wheel, instrument panel, and all the glass. And the black-on-yellow New York license plates are original to the car. Now that's amazing.

Paul was quite straightforward about the allure of unrestored collector cars: "They're only original once. Cars like this have no plastic or Bondo on them, and no restoration can duplicate an original car in good condition."

The condition of this Packard's interior must be seen to be believed. The upholstered door panels are perfect, the chromed handles remain free of any tarnish, and the finish on the wood trim and door cappings hasn't cracked. In fact, they still shine like new. And the seats appear as if they've seen very little use.

The dashboard looks as if a Packard factory worker just installed it. All the instrument faces look brand new, the chrome bezels and trim lack any pitting, and every switch and button below is just about perfect. Even the woodgrained dashboard and the top trim piece are well preserved. And the shifter knob shows almost no wear; neither does the Packard sill plate.

While the factory-applied lacquer paint is a little dull in places, and there are several chips and scratches here and there, every square inch of the body is just as Packard made it. Year-correct license plates and an old AACA (Antique Automobile Club of America) Greater New York Region badge lend this handsome sedan a period touch of authenticity.

Chapter 2

Pebble Beach Treasures: Preservation Class Entrants

I f you own a car that's been invited to take part in the Pebble Beach Concours d'Elegance, then you know all too well how special it truly is. While the world's finest restored classics take center stage, it's the Preservation Class, featuring some of the rarest and most desirable all-original collector cars, that has been gaining the attention of everyone of late.

As one would expect of Pebble Beach, where else would you find a completely original 1933 Duesenberg Speedster sitting near an equally original 1928 Stutz or 1932 Alfa Romeo 6C 1750? But that's what awaits you in the Prewar Preservation class.

Over at the Postwar Preservation through 1967 class, seeing a Jaguar C-Type and D-Type parked alongside an XK-SS, all three of which are as original as the day they rolled out of the Browns Lane factory, is a sight to behold. Recognizing the intrinsic value of unrestored automobiles, and parking them hand in hand with the finest in concours restoration, is the hallmark of an understanding organization that leads instead of follows. That's what makes the Pebble Beach Concours the greatest show on Earth.

Even with its French blue paint peeling off in several spots, revealing its hand-formed aluminum coachwork below, classic car collector Jacques Harguindeguy was proud to show his unrestored 1951 Delahaye 235 Saoutchik Cabriolet for all to admire in the newly created Postwar Preservation class at the 2007 event.

Concours Conservation

Preservation plays a particular part at the Pebble Beach Concours d'Elegance.

One of just a handful built by noted Italian coachbuilder Vignale, Jack Thomas entered his 1955 OSCA Vignale Berlinetta in the Postwar Preservation class in 2007. This hand-built coupe still wears its black lacquer paint quite well, and all of its engine components and interior details, including its Nardi wood steering wheel, are finely preserved with a welcoming patina.

Perhaps the most coveted Jaguar of all time, not only is an XKSS a rare sighting, but to see one in its original as-Jaguar-built-it state is an exceptional occasion indeed. Of the 16 XKSS models built, this 1957 example is one of at least two that are known to be totally original. Thanks to owners John and Heather Mozart for displaying it at the 2007 Concours.

RESTORATION PERFECTION has long been the key to the success of the Pebble Beach Concours d'Elegance. The automobiles that are invited for display on its legendary lawn can truthfully be considered the best of their breed. Their precise bodies, flawless paint, unblemished upholstery, and perfect plating will shock your senses silly if you've never seen such perfection before.

Conversely, so too will the cars in the Preservation classes. While there are thousands of well-kept original cars hidden away in garages throughout the world, what separates the unrestored beauties at Pebble Beach from all others is their incredible rarity. To possess both originality and rarity makes for a legitimately extraordinary automobile, hence their rightful place at the world's greatest concours.

As the leader in promoting the unmatched beauty of vintage originality, the Pebble Beach Prewar Preservation class has been gaining in popularity these last few years as more and more enthusiasts and collectors have come to recognize the significance of old cars in their natural, factory-assembled state. As a result, the concours committee added a second Preservation class at the 2007 event for "newer" cars, which is appropriately called "Postwar Preservation through 1967." Just as expected, this new class was a huge hit with both experts and spectators.

The Prewar Preservation class usually has about a dozen unique entrants, some of which are special-bodied one-off creations by the world's greatest coachbuilders; others are simply production-based classics. Seeing an unrestored Duesenberg speedster or Lincoln LeBaron sedan sitting alongside a Zagato-bodied Alfa Romeo 6C 1750 or a 500K Mercedes-Benz makes for a truly special experience.

Now that the cars from the 1950s and 1960s have taken center stage in the collector-car hobby, the time was ripe for a Postwar Preservation class. In its first year, seven cars took part in this momentous occasion, three of which were for display only. It was tough to say which unrestored car was the center of everyone's attention: the 1950 Ferrari 166 MM or the 1957 Jaguar XKSS. Perhaps it was the Jaguar C-Type or the D-Type. Maybe it was the Mercedes-Benz 300 SL coupe, the 1951 Saoutchik-bodied Delahaye, or the 1955 OSCA Vignale Berlinetta. As you can see, the cars that make up this class really are special, and as word spreads, there's no doubt that this class has the potential to be one of the most popular in the future of this spectacular event.

Eighty-seven years old and still running strong, thanks to the uncompromising construction quality and fine engineering that made Pierce-Arrow America's greatest motorcar, this 1919 Model 48 Touring car is a genuine example of the breed. Owner Patrick Craig treated show-goers at the 2006 Concours with the opportunity to view up close the intrinsic beauty of this original prewar touring car.

Only at Pebble Beach will you get to view an 1897 Henriod Duc Kellner Phaeton. Entered in the Prewar Preservation class by Roy Fisher of the United Kingdom, this remarkably original automobile celebrated its 110th birthday when displayed at the 2007 Concours. The original black paint had dried and cracked, the brass components had tarnished, and the wood artillery wheels turned black, but what an incredible piece of untouched automotive history it is.

At the 2007 Concours, Mark Smith exhibited his magnificent 1932 Chrysler Imperial LeBaron Roadster. This racy beauty is as fine an unrestored example of prewar Chrysler craftsmanship as one is ever likely to find. From its black exterior to the inviting worn leather upholstery to its stained canvas top, every square inch of this classic roadster is as original as the day it was first assembled.

With the paint on its hood rubbed down to the primer below, the nickel plating on the radiator surround and headlamps tarnished dull, and its interior showing years of lovable use, Wayne Herstad's 1923 Locomobile was a fascinating draw to the Prewar Preservation class in 2007. This original Model 48 Sportif has survived well, a testament to its high-quality construction and selection of materials.

In 2006, Daniel Brooks had his 1927 Voisin C11 Letourneur et Marchand Torpedo shipped over from London to enter it in the Prewar Preservation class. Nearly 80 years of use took its toll on the body; yet, although the paint has seen better days, from its delicate wheels to its large wood steering wheel, it's still in remarkable original condition. Truly an extraordinary example of French automotive history.

Chapter 3

Factory Fins:
Unrestored Cars of the 1950s

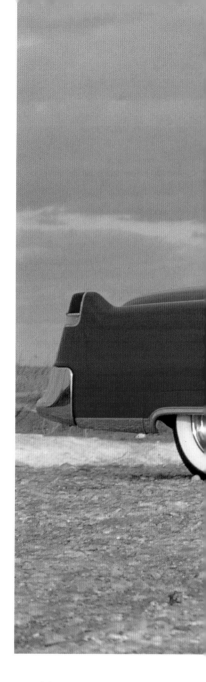

Big, bold, and achingly beautiful, cars that were built during the 1950s were perhaps the best-built American cars of all time. Even if they weren't the fastest, best handling, or able to stop quickly, their over-built construction quality remains unsurpassed.

Hiding behind those large chrome grilles were structures that were designed and constructed like a Sherman tank. Their massive frames were overdesigned, their sheetmetal was thicker than coins, and they were outfitted with interiors covered in fabrics that were practically wearproof. Those complex grilles and colossal bumpers were covered in thick layers of chromium and most had acres of side trim that was stamped out of corrosion-resistant stainless steel. Clearly, these are the main reasons why so many cars from the 1950s have survived without needing to be restored.

Practically every unrestored 1950s-era car that I've come across in my search suffered many of the same problems. Because the paint applied to cars back then wasn't nearly as hardwearing as the urethane enamels of today, and because they had shapely fenders, especially in the rear with their pronounced wings, the paint all along the topside was usually worn down to the reddish brown primer layer below. The same happened to the leading edge of the rounded areas of the hoods, both front and rear. Dashboards were painted then, and with their sliding heater controls nearly all had scratches in this area after years of use. And as for that aforementioned interior fabric, most examples had driver's-side door panels that were just plain dirty from being rubbed by the driver's left arm, yet none showed any tears or rips.

Cars of the 1950s are perhaps the most cherished cars of all time, which is why so many of them have survived in remarkable condition. This 1955 Cadillac sedan from Massachusetts is one such outstanding example.

The owners of 1950s cars seem more sympathetic toward their cars than do owners of other types of cars, which has resulted in a considerable number of these cars being saved from unnecessary restorations and repaints. Unfortunately, most of the more desirable models, such as the hardtops and convertibles, have already been restored, customized, or hot rodded, which is why most that remain in original condition are of the four-door sedan variety. Still, the fact that many of these four-door finned beauties still exist in such well-preserved states demonstrates the deep appreciation their owners have for them. And the collector-car community is all the richer because of it.

Imposing Imperial

Great deals, like this low-mileage 1950 Chrysler,
are usually found right in your own backyard.

HOW MANY TIMES have you seen a handwritten notice pinned to a bulletin board listing a car for sale, ripped off one of the tabs on the bottom with the seller's phone number, and promptly lost it by the time you got home or just didn't bother calling at all? If Dan Buckley of Shrewsbury, Vermont, had ignored an ad like that, he never would have found this unrestored Imperial that had been driven a scant 20,000 miles during its 57-year existence.

"There was a flyer for it hanging from the cash register at the barber shop when I went in for a haircut," Dan mused. "The flyer stated 20,660 original miles and the asking price. I bought it from the second owner who had acquired it somewhere around 1965. It had about 18,000 miles on it when he got it. He thinks the original owner lived in Flushing, New York, and was the prototypical old lady who only used the car to go to church and on other rare occasions."

Upon close inspection, the "little old lady" theory seems plausible. Looking closely at dashboard details and the interior upholstery during our enjoyable drive to a nearby photo location bears this out. Everything is so well kept it's easy to visualize someone's Aunt Millie behind the wheel. The gray mohair with blue leather upholstery and headliner are almost perfect, although the once-blue horsehair carpeting has faded to a lifeless gray tone.

Dan went on to say that there are a few problem areas. "The top of the rear armrest has fabric missing and the foam has cracked from the exposure to the light," says Dan. "There's a small mouse hole—which normally can't be seen—on the bottom of the driver's-side seatback where the armrest goes up and down. The material on the seats does not appear worn but seems to have 'shades' from sitting in the same position for so many years and having the sunlight hit the car through garage windows in the same path. The interior has been vacuumed numerous times and sprayed with odor killers to get rid of the mild mold and mildew odor that comes from being closed up for so long. I have been reluctant to use upholstery cleaner for fear of doing damage, but will try it on the seats in the spring when I take the car out of winter storage and do a cleanup. I have cleaned and polished all the interior chrome and metal using various hand tools as necessary, such as small brushes, to remove the layers of dirt or film when present and to get in all the little corners.

"Maintaining the car's original Shell Grey paint takes a lot more care," notes Buckley. "It was extremely dull, severely oxidized, and dirty. There are some thin spots where the primer is starting to show through, which makes wet sanding and buffing out of the question. I have been using a mild paint cleaner/polisher diluted further with paste wax and applied with a light-duty buffer and, of course, hand application in small areas and hard-to-get-at corners. I chose to go the route of repeated applications rather than use an abrasive polishing compound. There are some small scratches and chips that will need to be addressed to prevent future problems. The chrome

Large and spacious, the cavernous interior is completely as-assembled by Chrysler. The doors' mohair upholstery and grained vinyl inserts are flawless, although the color has faded a bit. The seats have held up remarkably well, and both the alabaster steering wheel and ashtray in the rear still look new.

has various levels of pitting but will not be touched."

Below the big hood resides the original 323.5-ci Spitfire straight-eight engine. This modest-size 135-horsepower flathead has had its original single-barrel carburetor rebuilt and the car's brake booster, brake master cylinder, wheel cylinders, brake shoes, tires, spark plugs, distributor, coil, points, ignition wires, thermostat, and water pump have all been replaced. But nothing needed to be done to the robust Prestomatic Fluid–drive four-speed automatic transmission.

"I like most things about the original nature of the car," Dan said. "There are factory inspection stamps on the firewall and part of a factory "OK" inspection sticker. Everyone that sees the car is fascinated by the inspection marks. The steering wheel is in pristine condition, as is all the chrome on the inside. All the door seals and rubber are in great shape with the exception of the trunk seal that I had to replace. I like the fact that some of the glass has small separations; it's like patina on an antique piece of furniture. There are no squeaks or rattles and the car rides smoothly like it did when new. The steering is tight with no play, but due to the early design it's very sensitive to crown on our dirt roads and side roads."

When I pressed Dan about the significance of original cars verses restored cars, his well-thought-out response was based on experience. "Original cars are more desirable because of the story that goes with them, where they came from, and the history of that particular car as well as the make and model. I like the idea of the rarity of finding something that has been preserved in its original condition and has been rela-

tively unused. Part of the problem with restored cars today is that the current standard is to restore cars to better-than-new condition, which causes the prices to be over the top. My 1961 Thunderbird is a good example. We use it a lot every year, which is reflected in the 121,000-plus miles on it. It is not perfect, and if it were, it would mean that I would not be driving it."

Everything inside the big 323.5-ci Spitfire flathead remains untouched, aside from the single-barrel carburetor that had to be rebuilt after years of sitting; now the six-cylinder powerplant functions perfectly smooth. All the factory-installed wiring, clamps, hoses, cables, and decals are still in place, and several "OK Paint" stamps are still clearly visible atop the firewall.

The perfectly preserved instrument cluster shows an odometer that has yet to reach 22,000 after almost 60 years, and every gauge still functions well. The glove-box trim has remained in alignment with the dash trim, instilling the occupants with that Imperial quality these conservatively styled cars were known for.

Worn but Wonderful

Warts and all, this 1950 Lincoln Sport Sedan still provides reliable service with unmatched behind-the-wheel enjoyment.

"THAT'S 1950 PAINT," said Jim Rawling, the incredibly proud owner of this very distinguished-looking Lincoln. "It's a pretty affordable car that's in really solid condition. I've been a Ford guy for many, many years—Lincolns, Fords, and Mercurys. I thought I deserved to drive something top of the line like the Cosmopolitan, but this is as close as I could get."

Jim runs a repair shop in Stephentown, New York, about 25 miles east of Albany, where he performs general mechanical repairs on both cars and trucks. The locals know him as the friendly mechanic with the old Lincoln. "It's my service car in the summer," Jim said. "If somebody needs a jump, I'll throw my booster cables in the back, and some tools in case I find something I can fix by the side of the road, which doesn't happen too darn many times anymore."

One of the reasons this old Lincoln Sport Sedan has survived so well is because it's originally from North Carolina. It was brought to upstate New York in 1979, used for just a few years, then sold to a local teenager who left the car in his parents' garage when he went to California. Jim bought it after it had sat on jack stands for about 10

years. "I paid $1,500 for it and thought it was a damn good deal for a car in that condition. It's pretty much rust-free and original. It's got 35,572 on the odometer, but the odometer doesn't work."

To make the big four-door Lincoln roadworthy again, Jim had to replace a few parts; yet he was careful not to do too much repair work that would otherwise take away from the car's original appeal. After performing a much-needed valve job, he painted the engine the proper shade of light green, the same color used on flathead Ford truck blocks. Jim purchased a replacement voltage regulator at his local parts store, along with rebuild kits for the brake wheel cylinders. The old bias plies were shot, so they were replaced with a set of modern radial tires. Unfortunately, the original hubcaps had rusted beyond use: a set of mid-1950s Cadillac wheel covers have been put on for now. Jim said that the car now drives and handles far better with the radials, and stops with authority.

Unlike other unrestored cars, the paint has seen far better days. There's primer showing through in many areas, and on the passenger-side front fender there are lots of rust patches. All the emblems and most of the exterior trim have that time-worn patina, the kind of weather-worn surface that makes these original beauties so appealing. The corner of the vent window glass

With the 152-horsepower 336.7-ci flathead V8 and original, factory-fitted Olds four-speed Hydra-Matic running as strong as ever, it's no wonder people in other cars are startled every time Jim goes blasting by. With its distinctive round headlamps and taillamps, this well-used Lincoln still turns heads wherever it goes.

The heavily tarnished front hood emblem has been transformed into a unique piece of automotive jewelry. A period-correct North Carolina license plate provides the crowning touch to a car that can't be mistaken for anything but all original.

and the glass on the split windshield has delaminated, yet they're still very much useable. All the proper switches, knobs, and gauges on the dashboard are original to the car and still work well, including the pull-out control keys for the heating system. As for the upholstery, the door panels are original, albeit in a nicely worn condition with just a few rips; the seats were reupholstered some 25 years ago and can now be mistaken for being original.

"I'd like to do the body over and repaint it, but it won't be affordable unless I do it myself," Jim said. "However, I really do enjoy it as it is. When I drive through the towns, old people and young people both say to me, 'I love your car.' It's a strange-looking car, or at least the nose is. But it's an original car, and I think people respect that. I can park it anywhere and never have to worry about the body getting dinged or the paint getting chipped. The car's much more enjoyable to use the way it is."

The interior may be worn, the seats ripped, the door panels stained, and the windshield delaminated in places, yet it remains an inviting and comfortable cabin for its appreciative owner.

Stately Motoring

Touring the country in a 1951 Nash Ambassador just the way the factory built it.

ARIZONA AND Southern California may get all the credit for being the land of rust-free cars, but if you have ever been to the desertlike high plains of eastern Oregon then you know all too well just what a goldmine this area is when it comes to vintage tin. With its relatively dry, warm climate, the town of Bend can be considered the gateway to this land of rust-free cars, and that's where this 1951 Nash Ambassador Super had resided through most of its existence.

Joining car clubs offers many benefits, especially when it comes to finding that particular car of your dreams via their classified ad listings. This is how Don and Lois Rancatti of Williamstown, Massachusetts, found this unmolested mint-green Nash four-door sedan. Showing slightly more than 35,000 miles on its odometer, practically every single aspect of this great American independent is original, including most of its exterior paint and interior upholstery.

Not one to place the car on a pedestal, Don and Lois regularly take long drives in the car whenever the weather is sunny and dry. In fact, Don enjoys driving his Nash so much he's driven it from his home in the Berkshires to the Stowe Classic Car show in northern Vermont with nary a single hiccup encountered along the way. After his drive, he told me, "With its soft wool and subtle vinyl gray and maroon upholstery, it's extremely comfortable and easy to drive. The 235-ci straight-six, overhead-valve engine puts out a very smooth 115 horsepower. It's adequately powered and gas mileage is good with the single-barrel Carter YF carburetor returning 22 miles per gallon on average. Thankfully, the three-speed Borg-Warner manual transmission does have overdrive, which helps. The brakes and steering are excellent considering lack of power assist."

During the two years that Don has owned this distinctive-looking Nash, he has had to replace a few parts to keep it roadworthy. Aside from the usual tune-up components and new tires, both front and rear bumpers had to be rechromed. Yet a part as simple as the heater's fresh-air filter has proven almost impossible to find.

"Considering the car's 57 years old, what I like most about it is its original paint," Don was proud to say. "Although when I display my Nash alongside other vehicles that are fully restored, the temptation to restore it is forever present. That is perhaps the most difficult aspect of owning such an original car. I know everyone says it, but cars like this really are only original once."

Besides its remarkable originality, Don went on to say about his Ambassador, "It's a reasonably rare automobile that's quite interesting. The workmanship on this Nash rivals the more expensive Cadillacs of this era." And that's a statement that shouldn't be taken lightly, as Don also owns not one but two 1949 Cadillacs.

Thanks to Nash's high build quality, the only major work needed on this robust engine was rebuilding its generator and water pump, yet all of the factory wiring still functions without problems. The sheet-metal-shaped engine bay, including the inner fender wells and the crossmembers that make up the Nash's unibody structure, is completely free of rust and still sports the factory-applied finish. The same goes for the rear shock towers.

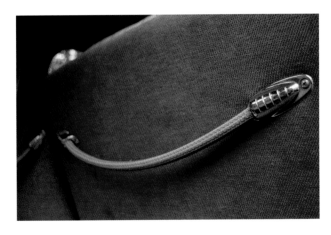

The big steering wheel, needed to offset the lack of power steering, has remained crack-free after nearly 60 years of use. The upholstery materials that Nash used throughout its interiors have proven durable, not to mention highly attractive. All the door locks and window winders still operate as-new smooth. Apart from some minor pitting of the chrome trim, the dash looks like it was just assembled, and the radio still provides clear reception.

Other than its distinctive bathtublike styling, the Ambassador's exterior design is fairly conservative, which is evident in its adornment. Aside from some slight pitting of its chrome plating, all of the brightwork has held up extremely well. And even though there are a few places where the paint has worn down to the primer below, its body and overall original condition are remarkable.

The Green Hornet

From the garage of its original owner emerged this very authentic 1954 Hudson Hornet convertible.

IMAGINE BEING SO LOYAL to a car that you keep it for more than 50 years, yet you drive it so infrequently you barely average 300 miles a year? Well, this attractive 1954 Hudson Hornet convertible is such a car, having led a very charmed life thanks to its faithful first owners. When purchased by second, and current, owner Peter Brown of Rye, New York, in 2006, a mere 15,000 showed on its odometer.

Peter, who is a national director of the Antique Automobile Club of America, was amazed at the Hudson's originality. "In my 45-plus years of collecting, this was the first top-of-the-line convertible that I had ever found

in this condition. Cars like this come along once in a collector's lifetime."

As one would expect from such a low-mileage car that had been babied and garaged all its life, it required almost no work. Due to its limited use, Peter took precautions and had the gas tank removed and boiled clean and had new brakes installed along with fresh fluid. Oh, and two power-window cylinders were frozen and both the clock and radio had to be repaired. Bodywise, there was a small dent in the driver's-side door that was repaired, as was some of the stainless-steel trim. And because a previous repair on the passenger-side door from the mid-1970s was beginning to show through, Peter had that section repainted.

But all else on this time-capsule Hornet is as Hudson built it. The canvas convertible top, burgundy leather upholstery, door panels, carpet set, paint, and plating are bone-stock factory original. And when combined with all the desirable options that Hudson owners crave, such as the Twin H package, automatic transmission, wire wheel hubcaps, power windows and top, compass, license plate holder, and curb signals (better known as feelers), you end up with the perfect recipe for the perfect Hudson.

Besides the aforementioned minor repairs, the only other item that required attention was the cleaning of the interior. After he had given the leather a thorough cleaning, Peter remarked, "You would think that over the years the leather would dry out, but it didn't. There was a little shrinkage in the back, but it was barely noticeable. Yet the most difficult part of maintaining the car's originality was that I had to be extra careful to preserve what I had without taking anything away from its condition, and that meant being especially careful during the cleaning process."

Since the old Hornet has been made safe for regular, reliable use, whenever the sun shines Peter takes it out for a spin just for the fun of it. "The way it drives and holds the road is what I enjoy most about this fabulous car," Peter said. "Before this, I had never owned a Hudson. I can do speeds of 70-plus and hardly feel it. They were way ahead of their time.

"If you can find an original car like this, there is nothing like it. Especially when nobody has messed with it. Because, as we have all heard many, many, times, they are only original once."

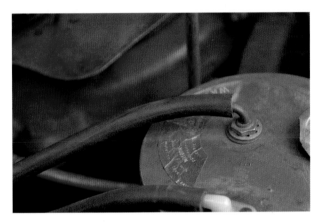

Generator, starter, radiator hoses, spark plug wires. They're all the original parts that were attached to this engine when it was new. Driven just 15,000 miles, the 308-ci straight-six has never needed any work: its Twin H carburetor setup has never gone out of tune, and its aluminum flathead has never warped.

The original white mark that some Hudson worker scribbled on the firewall is one of many details that have survived well on this remarkable automobile. So, too, did the glass windshield washer fluid container and its blue paper sticker that's still affixed to its aluminum top. Even the yellow decal detailing tire pressure and engine fluid information is still readable, albeit somewhat scratched.

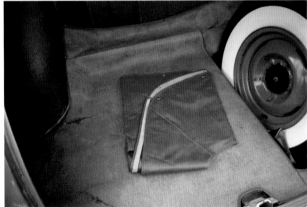

The chrome plating that Hudson used on its bumpers was of the highest quality—there's little noticeable pitting or tarnish present. All the stainless trim still buffs up to a brilliant shine and the original canvas convertible top continues to amaze everyone who sees just how well it has survived.

Durable leather has held up extremely well and still remains soft. Everything on the dash functions as it should; the big red steering wheel, its center emblem, and the speedometer are in perfect condition. The rear-seat upholstery shows almost no wear, although the driver's-side door trim wasn't so lucky. And the tissue dispenser slides out as smoothly as the day it was first installed.

Big Red

Living the good life behind the wheel of an all-original 1955 Cadillac Series 62 sedan.

"WHY NOT OWN 'The Standard of the World.'" It's a simple desire, especially if you've already owned a Cadillac before. Unlike many men his age, Alden Pierce of southeastern Massachusetts is attracted to big 1950s Cadillacs, more specifically, the Series 62 four-door sedan models. "I happen to really like cars from that era," Alden said. "I find nothing whatsoever exciting about today's cars; they're all just too bland and nondistinctive. I'm partial to sedans, even though I know they don't bring big money, but I like having rear access to the car's interior without having to tip the seat forward and squeeze inside."

Besides Cadillac sedans, Alden specifically prefers cars that are as original as possible. He previously owned a green, all original, 1955 Cadillac Series 62 four-door sedan, but it wasn't in as good condition, which is why he sold it. He said, "This red and beige car was in much, much better condition. Plus, red is my favorite color for a car. Coincidentally, this car just happened to be the same age I am. Perhaps that's why I was always attracted to cars from the 1950s, particularly the shapes and styles of 1950s-era Cadillacs.

"I found this car on eBay back in October 2003 and had to travel to New Castle, Pennsylvania, to get it. When the seller first pulled it out of the garage, the car was all dirty just from the garage being dirty, but I could tell that it was all there and structurally sound. Then I looked at the mileage, and looked inside, and realized it had to be actual. It only took me a couple of minutes to determine that this was something special, an actual low-mileage car. The interior was like a brand-new car; the pedals weren't even worn. It just needed a good cleaning.

"The seller was a nephew of the original owner, who I think was a lawyer, who operated his office out of his house and never drove anywhere, maybe 1,000, 2,000 miles a year. The nephew also had a 1953 Eldorado that he was keeping for himself. Between the two cars, I don't think they had 70,000 combined miles. I suspect the car spent at least one winter outdoors, because the roof has pockmarks, which probably came from having a tarp over it that the wind started flapping around. Also, there's a place on the side of the hood that could use some paint, but it's really not that bad. I'm not going to start touching it up because I don't want to interrupt its originality."

One of the first things Alden had to do was replace the original dry-rotted tires with a set of new Goodyear wide whitewall radials. All new tune-up components, radiator and heater hoses, battery, filters, fluids, a couple of light bulbs, and an entire exhaust system is all that was needed to make the big Cadillac roadworthy.

A look into the Cadillac's limited-use history is revealed on the oil-change stickers that are still stuck on the doorjambs. One sticker shows an 11,000-mile service in 1964, while a second sticker reveals an oil change in 1972 at 18,000 miles. Having been driven so few miles and being the recipient of such lavish care, the 250-horsepower 331-ci V8 engine purrs as sweet and smooth as the day it was bolted together.

"Restored cars are great, but there's nothing like an original unmolested vehicle," Alden said. "Besides, original, low-mileage cars don't come along every day—this car is a time capsule from 53 years ago. With my Cadillac, I feel like I am the custodian of an unusual vehicle, where it is my duty to keep it in good condition and retain as much of its originality as possible so that future generations can see an original car."

While protecting the Cadillac's freshness is his main priority, Alden still wants to enjoy the car by driving it. "My goal is to maintain the car's originality and keep it forever. It's only been driven 26,350 miles, and I add about 1,000 miles every summer. It's like I'm driving the same car as if I walked into a Cadillac showroom in 1955," Alden said. "I'm figuring that by the time it gets to the point where I finally kick the bucket, it might have 50,000 miles or so. Until then, driving this car never fails to make me smile. I love it."

Everything on this 331-ci engine is original, including the generator, starter, and water pump. The block, valve covers, and air cleaner assembly still wear their factory-applied paint, and will remain that way regardless of their scratches and exposed bare metal spots to preserve the car's originality.

To maintain the Cadillac's original factory finish, Alden bought a Porter Cable Polisher that he uses with Mother's Power Polish. He said that it really helped remove the oxidized top layer and brought back the bright red color. The chipped paint and tarnished trim adds a kind of character that can never be duplicated.

Sure, some of the chrome trim that adorns the decorative dashboard has tarnished and there are a few scratches on the painted section. Nevertheless, the overall appearance is that of a car that has been used sparingly since new.

The brown and beige upholstery is in remarkable condition, especially in the back, where very few people ever sat. The original door panels, robe strap, and carpeting look like they were just installed, and no cigarettes have ever stained the ashtray.

Green Mountain Cruiser

Enjoying the past with family and friends in a genuine 1955 Willys Deluxe Sedan.

OWNING AND MAINTAINING the factory-freshness of an original Chevy or Ford takes work, but if that unrestored car is a 1955 Willys Deluxe Sedan then what was considered to be a fairly routine chore of careful maintenance suddenly becomes a relentless exercise of cautious care and unyielding protection. There are no reproduction parts available for this particular model of Willys sedans, nor can parts be readily found for sale to provide you with backup body and trim parts. It isn't easy owning a car like this, especially one this original.

But if you're Charlotte Dayton of Leicester, Vermont, not only do you relish the task of maintaining such an unpolished gem—you constantly throw caution to the wind and drive it every chance you get. Even though it has only been driven a little more than 32,000 miles since new, Charlotte says, "We drive it as often as we can. I like this car because it's peppy, it's comfortable, easy to fix, good handling, and when you're on the road it's like being on your big old couch. Most of all, I like it because it's unique and different. That's why I drive it as much as possible, regardless how many miles I may add to it every year."

After Charlotte's husband and son drove the car back from Colorado, where it had lived in the dry climate

since the 1970s—clearly the reason why it is so well preserved—her goal was to keep it in top shape, both running and appearancewise, while driving and enjoying the car. "Sometimes you have to make choices," she said. "But it has a Kaiser 226-ci flathead six-cylinder, so if it breaks down on the road, I can fix it, just like I've been doing for years. Mechanical parts are interchangeable with Kaisers and Henry Js, which we collect and drive also. It is unique in a plain fashion."

Although the paint, trim, interior, and mechanical parts are all original to the car, an electric fuel pump was added to help eliminate recurring vapor lock problems. Other than new tires, brakes, and exhaust system, the little Willys is basically in the exact state of originality in which it left the factory. And to preserve that originality, Charlotte had plastic covers fitted to the seats to ward off further wearing. While Charlotte and her family enjoy cruising through the scenic backroads of Vermont in the Willys, she washes and waxes it several times a year to protect the factory-applied paint. When it's stored during the long, cold Vermont winters, along with her family's eight Kaisers, dryer sheets and mothballs are added to the interior to keep the mice away.

"I intend to enjoy history while I can," Charlotte said. "I know at some point we will have to do some restoration work to keep it able to be driven, but in the meantime we will drive wherever and whenever we can and

share with other folks as much as we can a unique model of automotive history.

"It is unique to have a part of the past. Unrestored cars are just that—an untouched past. People need to make the decision for themselves as to whether to restore a car or not, and what your plans are—drive or trailer?"

To prevent the original upholstery from getting ruined, plastic slipcovers were custom fitted to the front and rear to provide permanent protection. The metal glove box still slides out easily, as do all the vertical levers on the original-paint dashboard.

Everything in the trunk is original to the Willys too, including spare tire, jack, and floor mat. The jet-inspired taillamp housing's chrome and plastic lens are both in perfect original condition.

Fabulous Four-Door

Rare finds, as this low-mileage, all-original 1957 Chevrolet 210 sedan proves, can still be bought at small local auctions.

AUCTIONS ARE EXCELLENT places to find original collector cars, especially the out-of-the-limelight small auctions that are held throughout rural America. It was at one such auction in central Pennsylvania that John Rosman of Middle Island, New York, ended up being the winning bidder for this 1957 210 four-door sedan. "The car just mesmerized me when I saw it," John said. "I don't truly know why."

Showing just 29,500 miles on its odometer, the numbers are easily believed when inspecting this Chevy's exterior paint and interior upholstery. The quality of the Onyx Black and India White paint is excellent and the seats, door panels, headliner, and sun visors are flawless. About the only sign of use is the chipped black paint of the heater and vent slide buttons. Even the floor mats are factory originals, and in perfect condition, too.

The reason the upholstery is perfect is because the car's first owner had plastic seat covers put on front and rear; it wasn't until John bought the car that the covers were removed. When he drives the car, John protects the seats by sitting on white towels to ensure the fabric won't wear and the dye from his clothes won't leave any stains.

"In 2007 I drove it from Long Island to Hershey to attend and enter the car in the AACA Fall Meet, where it was given its HPOF award," John said. "The trip was approximately 260 miles each way; the car drives tight and handles excellent."

Before he left for Hershey, new brake shoes and wheel cylinders were installed, along with a new fuel pump and fuel tank sending unit. An axle seal had to be replaced, and instead of buying a reproduction radiator, John chose to have the original radiator re-cored to keep all the part numbers corresponding with the car's build date. In fact, John made sure that all the replacement parts were original-equipment parts and not reproductions. He said, "This takes time and research, but it's worth it.

"Car buffs seem to flock around it and are amazed with the original condition of a car that is over 50 years old. When parked at a car meet, this car receives more accolades and more attention than many 1957 Chevys that have been restored, which it deserves. I appreciate restored cars—I own a 1963 Thunderbird Sports Roadster and a 1979 Dodge Lil Red pickup—but to me there's nothing nicer than a true original. They are getting hard to find."

The deep shine on its factory-applied black body indicates that this Chevy was fastidiously maintained. Even the white roof and rear coves look like the paint was just applied. And the chrome plating on the front and rear bumpers looks better today, more than 50 years after they were first plated, than new reproduction bumpers look.

Aside from some minor pitting and scratches, the dashboard has retained its factory-fresh appearance extremely well. Even the gray steering wheel has not a single crack in its rim; the rubber floor covering is not only original but it too shows absolutely no wear. The radio-delete plate is quite rare, confirming, along with the lack of power steering or brakes, that the car's first owner was very frugal.

The 140-horsepower, 235.5-ci Blue Flame straight-six engine, with its one-barrel Rochester carburetor, has never been opened for repairs. The same goes for the two-speed Powerglide transmission, which shifts as smoothly as the day it was first assembled. The optional oil filter looks new, but it was installed back when the car was new.

Because the seats were covered with plastic from the time they were new, the two-tone cloth and vinyl upholstery is spotless, as is the fabric on all four inside door panels. The headliner has remained soil free with not a rip in sight; the chrome plating on the dome lamp's bezel is perfect.

Original-production details are everywhere. The data plate on the firewall is still covered in the factory-applied orange primer and the doorjamb's paint runs proves that too much black was sprayed on. The green paint dab on the steering box proved that its bolts were tightened, while the olive green clip shows how and where the wiring harness was attached.

Sparkling Starfire

*Used, yet well preserved, a more original
1957 Oldsmobile 98 just can't be found.*

LOCAL WANT ADS, *Hemmings*, and the Internet are the usual methods of finding the car of your dreams. While they all work well, sometimes you have to go right to the source to find what you're really looking for, and usually at a far more affordable price. And that source is a simple one: little, local car shows that are right in your very own backyard.

This is how Gary DellaVecchio from Oxford, Connecticut, ended up buying this unbelievable, all-original, Jade Mist green, 1957 Oldsmobile 98 Starfire four-door sedan. "I met a fellow collector at an Oldsmobile Show in Connecticut back in 2004," Gary recalls. "His name is Bob Helstrom and he owns a collection of cars that included this 1957 Olds. He said he was selling it to raise money to buy a 1941 Oldsmobile convertible. So I went to take a look at it and fell in love with it. I love 1957 Oldsmobiles.

"This car was in excellent condition," said Gary. "The ivory white leather and green Tri-lock cloth material was in mint condition. It may need new carpets, but they are still in decent shape. A thorough detailing, new tires, and a tune-up is all it really needed. All the options worked, including the foot switch, power antenna, power windows, and four-way power seat, except the Wonderbar

radio, which I fixed. The seller also included many parts and dealer items including a dealer shadow box of the same car. It lights up and was on display in dealer showrooms back in the 1950s."

So smitten was Gary with his unrestored Olds 98, that he started doing research into the car's past. "The car has remained in Connecticut its entire life, which I still find hard to believe," Gary said. "I was able to trace this car all the way back to the original owner because his name was in the owner's manual along with his address. I was able to call him and arrange a meeting to show him the car he once owned. He also gave me a picture of the car back in 1957 at Yellowstone National Park with a bear attacking the car. Very neat."

With Oldsmobile's excellent 371-ci Rocket V8 under the hood, the four-barrel Quadrajet-equipped powerplant puts out a mighty 277 horsepower. During the 107,000 miles that this durable engine has traveled, it has needed no repairs apart from a new water pump and new belts and hoses that Gary replaced. It still runs smoothly, and the four-speed Jetaway Hydra-Matic transmission hasn't needed any mechanical repairs either, a testament to those fine Lansing-based engineers.

"This car remains almost exactly as when it was new in 1957," Gary was proud to say. "All of the original parts, options, and drivetrain are still working as perfectly as they did 50 years ago. I think this is one of the

The original 277-horsepower 371-ci Rocket V8 has been cleaned and detailed but never taken apart, and the four-barrel Quadrajet carburetor remains untouched as well. Inside the trunk all is original too, including the floor mat, spare tire, and jack. Factory literature adds to the car's appeal.

While the front carpets show their age, all the upholstery looks as if it was just stitched together. The back seat is showroom perfect. The Wonderbar Super De Luxe AM radio takes a while to warm up, but it still provides clear reception. And as you can see, the dazzling dashboard has not a spot of pitting.

best examples of that model, and in remarkable unrestored original condition. I really think this car should be in a museum it's so nice."

Owning these big 1950s-era Oldsmobiles isn't like owning the more popular Cutlass or 4-4-2. Reproduction body panels, such as fenders and quarter panels and most of the exterior trim pieces, are not being made for them. Although this may be obvious to many, Gary zeroed in on some of the truly hard-to-find parts that most people readily overlook. "Original spare tires are incredibly hard to find today, as well as the factory jacks and tire irons," he says. "Also, it's getting increasingly difficult to find a set of those very desirable spinner hubcaps, along with all the hubcap clips. Windshield washer bottles, mint dash pads, power antennas, and original owner's manual are the other items that will take time to locate. I try not to drive it a lot, but it is hard to resist, as it's so cool to drive."

Rarity of body panels aside, Gary enjoys driving his Oldsmobile to the tune of more than 600 miles every year. "In order to preserve the car's factory-applied paint, I wipe the body down after I come back from every drive," Gary said. "I clean the interior with warm water and use IBIX wax on the exterior; I usually wax the car every six months. And I change the oil and filter often in order to keep the lifters as quiet as when they were new."

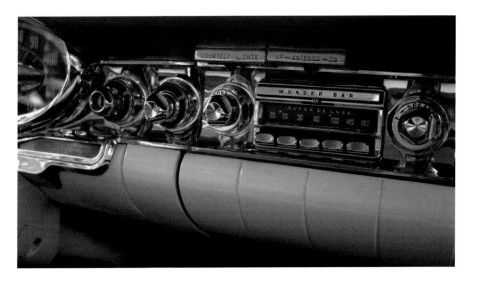

Keeping his Olds garaged all the time is the simplest way to ensure that its originality stays well-preserved. Gary knows he's fortunate to own such an original specimen. "There are very few original cars that are in really mint condition," he says. "To me, anyone who has the money or the talent can restore a car to mint condition. But to have an original car, well, sometimes you need to be at the right place at the right time and consider yourself very lucky to own one. I can't tell you how many restorers looked at my car in order to help themselves with their own restorations. So it's like having the cream of the crop. But truth be told, I bought this Oldsmobile to be a cruiser and not really to show it. Then I realized that this car was indeed special and decided to show it and enjoy its history. It just sort of happened. Now I search only for original cars."

Parked alongside his Olds is Gary's latest unrestored gem: a 1957 Chevrolet four-door sedan. It's an original power-pack car and still wears its original paint and interior. But at the time of my visit I wasn't able to photograph the car because Gary was in the process of cleaning and detailing the engine bay.

Gary gave me some good advice about finding these original automotive treasures: "You must take your time to find these types of cars. Original cars are special and you must look almost everywhere to find them. Stick with the old-timers. They have a lot of wisdom and they might just sell you that original car they love."

The big steering wheel hasn't a crack in sight, which is remarkable for plastic wheels of this era. Door panels show some water spotting and the painted window sill has worn mostly away, but that's to be expected after being driven more than 107,000 miles.

With its distinctive three-window design in the rear, this model Olds is loaded with unique design elements. Most of the stainless trim looks factory fresh, as do the still-perfect taillamp lenses; the chrome plating surrounding the exhaust outlets hasn't even tarnished.

Genuine Gems

One man's quest to build a significant collection of well-preserved originals.

SOME ENTHUSIASTS COLLECT CARS that were built in the year they were born; others specialize in one particular marque; some only want convertibles. For Joe Carfagna, a New Jersey salesman specializing in private aircraft, the primary focus of his growing collection is that of late 1950s and early 1960s American cars that are completely original.

From roaming the aisles at Carlisle to talking with car owners at Hershey to searching the classified ads in *Hemming Motor News* or his local Pennysaver, Joe is always on the lookout for old cars that are in original, factory-assembled condition. However, they must retain their factory-applied paint and upholstery, and must generally be in respectable condition overall.

At the AACA's fall meet in Hershey in 2007, Joe finally got the chance to buy a car that he's been chasing for years. When he saw it drive onto the show field at the start of Saturday's huge car show, he dropped what he was doing and went over to talk to the car's owner to see if he could buy it. And he did. Now, a one-owner, unrestored 1965 Pontiac Bonneville station wagon with its original silver-blue paint sits in Joe's garage.

"No matter how nicely you restore a car, you can't make it drive as well as a low-mileage original," Joe remarked To back up that claim, Joe decisively stated, "I love survivors! I never met one I didn't like."

1959 Oldsmobile Super 88

"Preservation and drive, drive, and drive," are the two main goals owner Joe had set for himself when he took possession of this highly stylish and exceptionally original Super 88 hardtop. "I always wanted a 1959 Oldsmobile two-door hardtop; I just love the styling and its two-tone color combination. Finally, in 1999, I found a really good one. I discovered this car listed for sale in *Hemmings Motor News*; it was located about a 16-hour drive north of my New Jersey home, in Ontario, Canada.

"The entire interior, including all the upholstery, door panels, and headliner are original. The original carpet is a little weak, but why change it? Only mechanical maintenance items have been replaced on this car; that's about it." The trunk mat, too, is the same mat that the Oldsmobile came with, as are the hard-to-find factory-issued spinner hubcaps.

Besides trying to maintain and preserve the quality of the original acrylic lacquer paint and two-tone interior, Joe said that "keeping gas in the tank!" is the hardest

part of owning this car. Evidently, the 394-ci Rocket V8 with its four-barrel Rochester carburetor isn't the most fuel-efficient engine in the world, which isn't helped any with the three-speed Jetaway automatic transmission that accompanies it.

This original engine and drivetrain has traveled some 56,000 miles, and have never been taken apart or needed any mechanical attention. Everything works as smoothly and reliably as the day the General Motors workers bolted everything together. To ensure everything stays well lubricated, Joe takes it out for a drive every few weeks. He adds a little over 1,000 miles to the odometer each year, and no matter where he drives, it always generates lots of attention.

The carpets may show some wear and the front seatbacks are a little dirty, but everything is just as it came from Oldsmobile. The upholstery in the rear is in spanking new condition and all four door panels look like they're only a few years old—not a half-century.

Most of its original green paint may have worn off, but the 394-ci Rocket V8 purrs along in a most aggressive manner; the yellow silkscreened filter instructions on the air cleaner assembly survived nicely. The black splotch on the firewall and overspray-covered body trim plate on top show how even back then work sometimes was done in a slapdash manner.

IMPORTANT ▶ REPLACE ELEMENT
NORMAL CONDITIONS— 10,000 MILES
DUSTY CONDITIONS— 5,000 MILES OR
WHENEVER VISIBLY WORN OR PLUGGED.
DO NOT WASH, OIL OR CLEAN WITH AIR HOSE
AC ELEMENT TYPE
A 44 C
MADE IN USA

The preservation of this Super 88's originality is remarkable. The insulating panels and tire-change instructions on the trunk lid as well as the floor mat and the matching cardboard panels surrounding the hinges are all in near-perfect condition.

1960 Mercury Montclair

Car clubs are one of the best resources when it comes to finding good deals on desirable collector cars. Every club, be it one that focuses on an entire brand or a particular model, publishes either a newsletter or a magazine that lists cars and parts for sale by its members. Many club members prefer to sell their cherished automobiles to like-minded enthusiasts, knowing full well that their car will be going to someone who truly appreciates the car for what it is, not how much it's worth.

As a member of the International Mercury Club, Joe found this Montclair listed for sale in the club's magazine in early 2007. "These Mercurys have great styling, but more than that they are very unusual," Joe said about his latest Mercury, one of three that he owns. "The car's condition is what I like best about this particular car. It came from Palm Springs, California, so it is perfect underneath."

The main attribute of this distinctively styled Montclair that got Joe's attention was its low mileage. With just 20,200 miles on its odometer, the fact that it resided in the dry West all its life and was almost 100 percent original meant that it was one of those welcomed opportunities that come along once in a lifetime. A rare find indeed, which is why Joe called the seller as soon as he spotted the ad.

Due to a somewhat minor dent and scrape along the passenger-side quarter panel shortly after Joe bought the car, this section of the body was repaired and color matched to the existing beige paint, all of which is original to the car. So, too, are the beige vinyl and cloth upholstery, brightwork, 430-ci V8, and Merc-O-Matic transmission. And all of it is incredibly well preserved for its age, thanks to the dry, warm climate of Palm Springs.

Big and powerful, and driven less than 21,000 miles from when it was new, the 430-ci V8 remains untouched. Even the gold air cleaner assembly and valve covers still wear their Mercury-applied gold finish.

Just what you would expect from a low-mileage car that resided nearly its entire existence in the dry climate of California: a body and interior that look as good as the day the car was first built. The carpet and doorjambs, the upholstery and trim—everything has been preserved in as-new condition.

1960 De Soto Fireflite

"What a great body style!" is Joe's reasoning for always wanting to own a 1960 De Soto.

Finished in the pleasing color combination of blue and white, this Fireflite is in virtually the same condition as when Joe found it in 1996. Apart from a thorough detailing and tune-up, the car needed very little. The factory carpet had to be replaced due to excessive wear—the previous owners had driven it 65,000 miles—and the automatic transmission was in desperate need of a rebuild to cure a heavy leak of its transmission fluid.

Loaded with goodies including swivel seats, dual antennas, power steering, and power brakes, the 361-ci V8 engine with its two-barrel carburetor is original to the car as is its push-button TorqueFlite transmission. In fact, almost every single mechanical and electrical component under the hood remains—and works—in outstanding form, just as De Soto intended them to last.

For a car as long and wide as this Fireflite, one would think that it would have accumulated some major battle scars after being out on the road for nearly a half century, but this De Soto has always been cautiously driven, well looked after, and garaged for safekeeping. Its interior upholstery is in very good condition with just a few spots of discoloration, the headliner is practically perfect, and every bit of trim throughout its dazzling dashboard is in equally fine shape. Minor scratches of the trim, inside and out, attest to its years of use but in no way detract from its originality. As for the paint, well, it too has withstood the test of time quite well. A thorough compounding and annual polish and wax are all that's needed to prevent the body from needing a respray.

Joe averages about 1,000 miles per year in his Fireflite, and says that he loves all the attention and positive comments he gets about the car's styling.

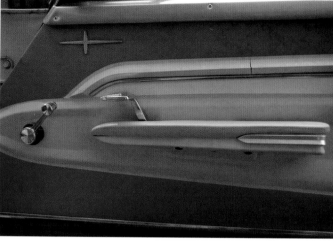

The eye-catching tritone upholstery and swivel front seats have held up well even after 65,000 miles of use. All the push-buttons on the symmetrical dash work and the road map compartment within the glove box appears to have never been used.

Showing that it had an oil change on 4/27/65 at 49,170 miles, the 361-ci V8 may not look like a well-maintained engine, but it is. Having retained all its original components, it still runs smoothly and is always reliable.

There are many design elements on the 1960 De Soto that make it vulnerable to damage, such as the protruding taillamps and unprotected grille, yet they are all in exceptional original condition, including the factory-applied light blue paint.

1962 Mercury Monterey

Similar to cars that have been restored, there are many different quality levels of originality. Some unrestored cars are clearly better than others, then there are those that are truly extraordinary; this is one of those cars.

About this Monterey, Joe said: "My absolute favorite thing is its condition. I bought it from the original owner who kept the car in incredible condition. He was very meticulous. It still rides like a new car."

Driven just 35,000 miles since new, Joe said that the big Mercury shows almost no wear at all. The tan vinyl upholstery is in fantastic shape as is the car's beige paint that was applied at the factory almost five decades ago. The 352-ci V8 engine and three-speed Cruise-O-Matic transmission still perform flawlessly; only the usual items that wear have been replaced. The glitzy-looking dashboard appears as if it were just assembled; both the headliner and carpeting appear factory fresh.

Finding a two-door Monterey hardtop in similar condition is almost impossible today, yet this car is proof positive that they're sill out there. "I have been looking for a '62 Merc for many years, and when this car was offered to me by its original owner I didn't think twice about buying it," Joe was happy to say. "I just love those 'flashlight' taillamps!"

The appearance of untouched original engines such as this Monterey's 352-ci V8 is a huge plus for collectors seeking original cars because they know it has never been messed with. The red plastic windshield washer fluid bag has survived the heat of the engine bay quite well. It appears that Mercury painted their hood springs red.

Besides its individualistic styling, the chrome plating on this uniquely designed taillamp is of the highest quality, evidenced by the lack of even a single pit mark. The same can be said about the decorative trim panel in the rear with its painted black background. All are finely crafted parts that have withstood the test of time very well.

When a car is owned by just one owner its condition is usually superior to those cars that have had multiple owners. Judging by this Monterey's flawless interior, perfect dashboard, and spotless two-tone upholstery, there are real advantages to possessing one-owner cars.

1964 Chevrolet Impala

If you're a serious car enthusiast living in the East, then no doubt you've attended Spring and Fall Carlisle. I know I have, many, many times. In fact, I started attending way back in the early 1980s. And every time I go to Carlisle, one of the first areas I head for is the car corral. Through the years I've seen several really good deals, mostly for cars that aren't on everyone's top ten list. Still, there are deals there to be had.

At Spring Carlisle 2004, Joe was walking through the aisles of the car corral when he happened upon this 1964 Chevrolet Impala convertible. Fortunately for Joe, it didn't look nearly as nice as it does here, which is why everyone else passed it by. This Impala was sitting there looking totally disheveled, yet Joe clearly saw through its grubby appearance. Evidently, the seller hauled it out of a New Hampshire barn where it had sat for 20-plus years; it was probably more like 30-plus years judging by the odometer's reading of a scant 11,000 miles. The car was very dirty and neglected and was being sold as is.

It's amazing how a thorough cleaning and detailing can transform a car from total dog to amazing beauty queen. "This Chevy's incredible condition is what I like most about the car," Joe said. "And the way it rides is simply unbelievable."

Obviously, due to the car's limited use, everything on the car showed little or no wear. From the armrests and door panels to the carpeting and ignition lock, every component looks brand new, as if they were installed yesterday. In fact, even the convertible top is the very same top that was installed on the car at the Chevrolet factory where it was built. According to Joe, "There isn't much on the car that has been replaced. After I bought it, I put on new tires and had to replace all the hoses, belts, plugs, points, filters, and the muffler. Everything that I pulled off the car was factory original."

When I asked Joe to open the trunk, I just could not believe its condition. The splatter paint was in outstanding condition, as were the three floor mats; the surrounding weather stripping wasn't even ripped or dry rotted. Most amazingly, the spare tire is the original U.S. Royal whitewall that came with the car, with the original jack and tire iron carefully stored underneath it—its factory-applied GM instruction decal is in respectable condition, too.

Yet, the most exceptional items that came with the car are the pair of paper floor mats. For such throwaway items to not only exist for some 45 years but to have been kept in such perfect condition, with nary a rip or splotch of dirt on them, is totally unbelievable. Just being able to photograph them made my day.

"Original cars like this run so much better than restored cars," Joe told me with great enthusiasm. "The

only problem is that when you're driving it, which I only do about 300 miles at most per year, is making sure nothing happens to it. After all, it's probably the lowest-mileage 1964 Impala convertible in the world. That's why it has a particular place in my collection. I just love it. I plan on keeping it forever."

The 283-ci Turbo Fire V8 is still equipped with all the ancillary parts that were bolted to it at the factory. The inner fender wells are completely free of rust and still have the protective rubber flaps that cover the upper A-arms stapled to them. Even the glass windshield washer bottle, which usually broke early on, remains in fine condition.

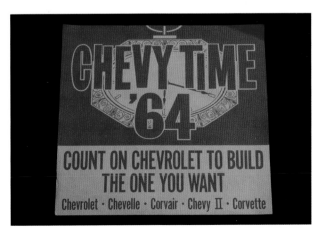

The interior on this Impala is simply unbelievable. Dirty when purchased, a comprehensive cleaning has revealed its immaculate original condition. Most amazing is the pair of perfectly preserved 1964-issued Chevy Time paper floor mats that the car's first owner saved. The nonoriginal seatbelts were recently added so Joe can take his kids driving with him.

Just as AMC assembled it—everything in this Gremlin's engine bay remains in as-built condition. Driven less than 4,000 miles, the 232-ci straight-six is barely broken in and still features its factory-installed radiator hoses and clamps.

The bare-bones interior features tough-wearing white vinyl upholstery and a one-piece rubber floor mat in place of carpeting—both are in excellent original condition. And the always-fragile rubber boot at the base of the stick shift has remained rip free.

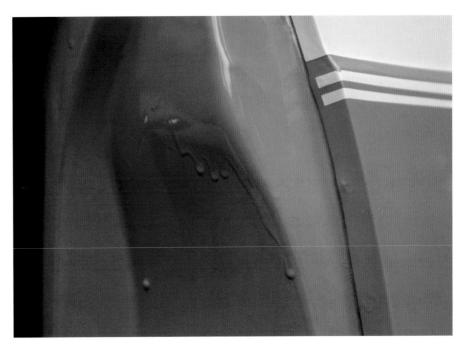

Two great examples for Gremlin restorers on how the cars were really built: Black overspray behind the headlamps proves that this area was painted after the body color was applied, and excess painting on the doorjambs resulted in numerous drips—seeing how the side stripe wraps around the panel edge is another factory trait that future restorers can learn from.

Symbolic Diplomat

*From Mexico City with love, this 1947
De Soto is now owned and cherished
by the son of the original owner.*

"I LEARNED A LOT about basic automotive mechanics on this car," longstanding owner and engineer Carlos Heiligmann told me when I visited him at his home in Rowe, Massachusetts, one sunny autumn day in 2007. "Not only did this De Soto introduce me to the antique car hobby, but it's a concrete and visible link to my past, especially to my formative years in Mexico."

Carlos' father bought this handsomely styled De Soto Diplomat four-door sedan, model SP-15C, new in Mexico City on December 6, 1947. He went on to say, "I 'took it' from him in the early 1960s. Actually, he gave it to me when I started to drive; he taught me to drive on this car. My first intention with the car was to have transportation in high school, college, and beyond, then it was to maintain the car in its original condition and maintain it forever."

If you think this De Soto looks more like a Plymouth than a De Soto, you're right. It's a rare export model that was built for markets outside of the United States. In addition to its Plymouth body, it incorporates Dodge details such as the front parking lamps, yet the body is wrapped by De Soto emblems and detailing. Its styling is quite unique.

The De Soto's 217.7-ci engine was also an export-only powerplant, meaning that it was originally engineered with a relatively low 5.6:1 compression ratio. Once Carlos had the car in the States, it was rebuilt with a slightly higher 6.6:1 ratio, allowing it to better cope with interstate travel. Although the three-speed manual transmission is standard for Mopars of this era, the export-only rear axle ratio is 4.30, which is substantially lower than the U.S.-spec 3.90 ratio.

One of the reasons this De Soto has been so well maintained is because Carlos' father, who was also an engineer, kept meticulous records. Carlos remembers, "My father was excellent with details, such as maintaining service records and keeping all the original manuals in excellent condition. The car has not been modified, so it still gives the original feeling of driving a car of this era." With such devoted care and strict attention to maintenance and repairs, it's no wonder this is one of the best-preserved 1947 De Soto sedans in existence. It really is a treat to sit inside this well-preserved time capsule, to experience the welcoming feel of the original pinstripe wool upholstery and appreciate not only the car's incredible shape but its international history.

Carlos said that the most difficult part of upholding the De Soto's originality is "maintaining the paint—its shine, integrity, color—in its original condition. Thankfully, the car is easy to repair and parts are usually available." After being exposed for more than six decades to the harsh sun, strong winds, acid rain, and airborne particles that are quite abrasive, the Gunmetal Gray exterior finish has a slightly dull appearance about it. But it's an honest finish, with nary a rust bubble or conspicuous scar found anywhere on its comely body.

As one would expect of an export model, there are several unusual components on the car that, today, are now considered quite rare. The two most obvious items are the metric instruments and the hood ornament. The speedometer is in kilometers and the temperature gauge readings are in Celsius. Other hard-to-find De Soto parts are the hubcaps, rear center stoplamp, the front grille, and all the stainless-steel moldings and trim.

The first thing that many people notice when they see the De Soto is the car's distinctive center opening doors, followed by the fine condition of the car's overall originality. The real treat, of course, is the metric dash, which everyone gets very curious about once they notice it.

In the 62 years that this metric speedometer has been functioning, it has recorded 142,900 kilometers, which translates to around 89,300 miles. Now this fascinating De Soto gets driven somewhere around 2,000 miles annually, but only during good weather, which here in the Berkshire mountains of western Massachusetts translates from April through October. Then, inside the garage next to his all-original 1973 Volvo 144, it sits until spring arrives again.

"Very few people know what the car really is," Carlos said. "They assume it is like the De Sotos they knew when they were children. It makes people very happy to see this car. Many are fascinated to learn of its history— it is sometimes called "a Plymouth in disguise" because it is a Plymouth body with De Soto markings. But the most desirable attribute of original cars like this De Soto is that they provide a valuable link to the past and that they maintain that link for generations to come. This car eventually will find a home in the Chrysler museum."

The rare accessory grille guard has protected the multifaceted grille well, while the quality postwar chrome plating has resisted pitting and still looks excellent. With all the trim looking new, along with the period plate, you would think this was 1947.

Anyone who sees this car's interior would have trouble believing that it had never been restored. The woodgrained metal dashboard is in exceptional condition as are all the gauges, including the export speedometer, which is in kilometers. The radio and speaker grille assembly (including each of the alabaster knobs below) and the Mopar Deluxe heater are all original and perfect.

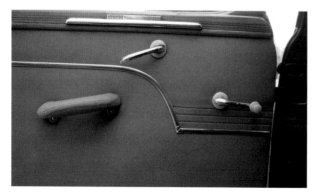

The interior is in overall excellent condition for its age, with only slight wear on the window sill where drivers' arms have rested all these years. The upholstery in the rear looks practically brand new, and although the headliner has minor water stains, it too remains in good condition and doesn't have to be replaced anytime soon.

The rebuilt 217.7-ci flathead-six is still equipped with its original single-barrel Carter D6G1 carburetor, as well as all of its other ancillary components, including starter and generator motors. This well-preserved air cleaner decal looks great for being more than 60 years old.

The original brass Direccion de Registro Federal de Automoviles data plate is still riveted in place and the Registrado window sticker from 1960–1961 has never been removed.

Photography courtesy of Greg Cockerill

Buick Brilliance

Driven less than 10,000 miles, if ever exists a "brand-new" 1960 LeSabre, this is it.

RARE IS THE ORIGINAL CAR that still wears all its factory-installed parts. Yet, every now and then one surfaces that puts all the rest to shame. This 1960 Buick LeSabre convertible is one of those atypical finds.

Like many cars no longer used once their owner dies, this Buick was stored in a garage in 1969 after its owner had passed away. Driven just 8,300 miles, the sentimental husband let the car sit there, unused, until he passed away in 1993. Shortly thereafter, it was bought by Greg Cockerill, a powertrain engineer at General Motors in Pontiac, Michigan.

Because his dad and favorite aunt both had 1960 LeSabres that were Artic White with red interiors, Greg wanted the same. But finding one that was unmolested was quite the challenge. "I was sick and tired of inauthentic and poor-quality restorations," Greg said. "The incredible originality and high-quality condition made this car a once-in-a-lifetime opportunity. It was like a time capsule, or the proverbial barn find. I was stunned that it still had the original factory tires. It's the closest thing to owning a new 1960 Buick, and better and more authentic than a restoration. The wonderful color combination was an added bonus."

The benefit of having been garaged in a cool climate has kept the interior in fantastic condition, and, most remarkably, the steering wheel is completely free of cracks. "However, there are some areas that show wear and age," Greg said. "The driver's-side carpet exhibits moderate foot wear, as the car apparently never had floor mats, and the pristine condition of the passenger- and rear-seat carpet confirms the car's life in a home without children. Also, there are some small areas on the door panels with black stain spots. Initially, I assumed it was mildew, but it's actually permanent staining from the factory adhesive on the backside of the vinyl that has leached through the material. It is a permanent discoloration, so we have learned to live with it."

"Owning a low-mileage 'survivor' is not for the casual collector," Greg stated. "The care and feeding that is necessary to preserve a car like this requires patience, dedication, and sacrifice. You must be prepared to let the weather limit your participation in shows, and be willing to search for months for exactly the correct mechanical part, instead of using easier-to-find generic parts. When driven, there's an ever present need to protect the original components so as to alleviate the need for future replacement or repair. This means being vigilant of all possible wear and tear, both cosmetic and mechanical, especially the fragile interior, and the largely irreplaceable exterior chrome trim."

Preservation is the key to maintaining a car's finish in its original state, which is why Greg is so fastidious about how his LeSabre is maintained. "The car is kept out of

There are several exterior parts rarely seen on 1960 Buicks that are still in place on this spectacular unadulterated specimen. The outside rearview mirror, radio antenna, rear license plate frame, and the salt-and-pepper carpet with correct seams are all perfect.

the sun as much as possible. Passengers must sit on white towels to prevent sweat stains or color transfer from their clothing, and the floor is covered with protective matting. After using the car, all interior chrome is wiped down for fingerprints. Periodically, the interior chrome is waxed and a thin coating of a Meguiar's protective vinyl product is applied to the seats and door panels, and all weather stripping is gently wiped with a silicone product.

"When I first got the car, I hand-rubbed the body with a gentle polish to remove old wax, dead paint, and light scratches. I spent months touching up paint nicks, creating the right amount of paint build-up to allow them to 'disappear' on the white surface," says Greg. "However, not all the imperfections could have been removed without losing the originality of the finish. Since then, the car is given a yearly coat of glaze by hand and the die-cast chrome pieces are protected with paste wax to help seal them from moisture and humidity. More importantly, the car is never washed, and has not seen water since I bought it; only a 'California Duster' is used. For winter storage, I place the car inside a sealed, humidity-controlled car bag."

Greg brought up some valid points regarding originality. "With a piece of fine art, an unmolested original is always more desirable and valuable than a restoration. Why has this not always been the case with cars? Until a few decades ago, great originals were merely considered a good starting point for a restoration. I'm personally pleased to see the explosion of interest in leaving unrestored cars in their original state. I think this

epiphany of the hobby towards preservation is partly due to an emerging recognition of the cars' historical significance, as well as the constant elevation of authenticity in judging. As usual, the trend has been led by the Corvette community, which was the first to coin the phrase 'survivor.' Club preservation classes for unrestored cars have been effective in promoting this part of the hobby, too. And there's the issue of rarity. As the cliché goes, a car can be restored over and over again, but is only original once. This makes an unrestored survivor a rare one-shot deal—either it's original or it isn't, and if it isn't, it can't be changed back."

A strong advocate for unrestored cars, Greg's other collectible is also an all-original Buick convertible: a Bamboo Cream 1970 Electra with only 39,000 miles on it; still, the LeSabre, which he drives about 400 miles annually, is his favorite. "This has been the most rewarding and fun-to-own collector car I've ever had. I like knowing that this was exactly the way it left the factory in 1960, the way it looked and drove. I'm preserving history for the future of the hobby and take pride in the fact that after nearly 50 years, this car is as close to a new 1960 Buick convertible as one could ever find. It's reassuring to know that I have an unmolested car that is above reproach in terms of being 'correct.' A side benefit that has provided great satisfaction is that I've been able to assist numerous 1960 Buick enthusiasts around the country with their restoration and technical questions. And it's a special point of pride for me when people ask about its 'restoration'—and are stunned to learn it's actually an unrestored car."

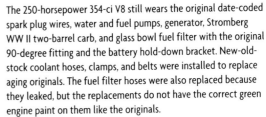

The 250-horsepower 354-ci V8 still wears the original date-coded spark plug wires, water and fuel pumps, generator, Stromberg WW II two-barrel carb, and glass bowl fuel filter with the original 90-degree fitting and the battery hold-down bracket. New-old-stock coolant hoses, clamps, and belts were installed to replace aging originals. The fuel filter hoses were also replaced because they leaked, but the replacements do not have the correct green engine paint on them like the originals.

With the original-equipment Delco spiral shocks still working well, the original tires and wheels were removed intact and saved. Another set of 1960 Buick wheels and correct repro BFG 7.60x15 bias-ply tires were installed, but the original spare still resides in the trunk, along with the original floor mat. All four T-3 headlamps are original and still work.

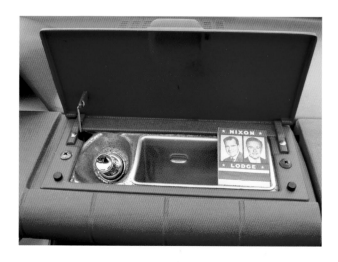

All of the die-cast trim and chrome-plated parts have remained free of pitting and are now protected with an annual coating of paste wax. They complement the perfectly preserved factory-original upholstery, door panels, and dashboard components. A new-old-stock map lamp was installed to provide courtesy lighting for the front-seat passengers, and the ashtray appears hardly used.

Original detailing like this is a rarity, even on well-maintained cars. Be it the painted hinges, numbers tag, lamp switch, or door panels, everything appears as if Buick just assembled it. Even the weather stripping hasn't dried out or cracked.

Cruising Crown

California to Connecticut and back in an unrestored 1961 Imperial Crown.

NOT MANY CARS can be close to a half-century old with over 185,000 miles, and still wear their factory-applied paint so well. And with each passing year another 2,500 miles gets added to this Imperial's odometer. But not during the summer of 2007: That's when Paul Graveline from Orangevale, California, decided to drive his big Chrysler across the country to attend his 50th high school reunion in Connecticut. But on the way he made a slight detour north to Vermont to visit *Hemmings Motor News*, arriving on the day of one of our cruise nights. By night's end, Paul took home the "Favorite Mopar" award because the *Hemmings* editorial staff not only appreciates these full-size cars but because Paul had the courage to do what many of us only dream of doing, and that's to cruise the entire country in our favorite collector car just for the fun of it. Paul did exactly that, and in a car that is not only rare but incredibly original, too.

Only 1,896 Imperial Crown two-door hardtops were built for the 1961 model year, and this just very well may be the most original example in existence—and the one with the highest mileage, too. Perhaps the biggest reason why there are so many miles on this stylish machine is because of the way it soaks up the irregularities of the road. According to Paul, "Aside from its looks, its ride is

what I like most. It's such a comfortable cruiser, and the Torsion-Aire suspension handles 5,000 pounds of moving automobile quite well, considering the vintage."

During his nearly 8,000-mile trip across the United States, Paul had a case of 104-plus Octane Booster in the trunk, added at each fill-up to ensure that the big 413-ci V8 wouldn't ping itself apart, especially when crossing the Continental Divide. The Mopar electronic ignition system that he installed prior to his big trip made a huge improvement in drivability.

If it's not raining, Paul takes the big Chrysler out for a drive every Sunday, and attends numerous car shows and cruise-ins. "My main objective is to maintain its originality, cruise in luxury, and enjoy it, which I have," Paul said. "Unfortunately, age and usage take its toll. Items wear and/or break. And the low production numbers for Imperials make finding parts difficult. Glass and all the outside trim on this car are rare and hard to find, but all of it is on this car and in good condition."

The front seat had been reupholstered in the correct white and gold broadcloth and vinyl material by the previous owner before Paul bought the car in January 1996. It had already been driven 117,000 miles by this point. The rest of the interior is completely original, but it does shows its age. The carpet is worn and the rear shelf material is heavily faded due to the harsh California sun and is falling apart. Although he's trying to maintain the car's originality as best he can, Paul said, "Eventually,

With its tall wings rising up into the airstream, nicks and scratches in the factory-applied paint have been far and few between. Most chips appear on the leading edge of the front hood and surrounding the gas-filler door. Most of the chrome plating still shines like new.

the interior will get so shabby that I will break down and redo it to original specifications."

Deep down, replacing the car's interior is the last thing Paul wants, saying he will hold off as long as possible. "An automobile is original from the manufacturer only once. It can be restored many times with reproduction or new-old-stock parts, paint, upholstery, etc. Bottom line: It's only original once."

Paul went on to say, "The main reason I purchased this particular vehicle was because of its uniqueness, styling, and features. It is the ultimate Virgil Exner styling on a mass-produced automobile.

"I'm a Chrysler product enthusiast," says Paul. "I also own a 1957 Imperial Crown four-door hardtop, a 1963 Chrysler 300 Sport, 1968 Newport convertible, 1970 Dodge Charger, and 1947 and 1973 Dodge pickup trucks. The Imperial is Chrysler's luxury brand, the best they had to offer. I have always loved their fin-era vehicles and to me the 1961 Imperial tops them all. Great fins, curvaceous sheet metal, generous chrome, and those pedestal headlamps and hanging taillamps—rolling automotive art!"

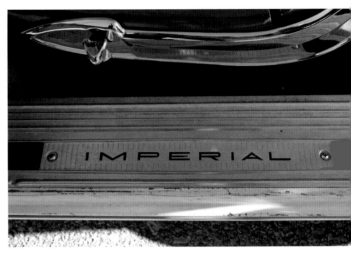

Maps, coffee cup, tissues, pens, and medicine were some of the many things needed regularly during Paul's 8,000-mile trip across the USA. Upholstery had been replaced years ago, but the carpets, headliner, rear seats, and the entire dashboard assembly are untouched originals. The Imperial sill plate is dull but not worn.

The upholstered door panels are still in fine condition, although the slightly worn armrest clearly shows the years of use it has endured. Lacing around the vent windows may be torn and tattered but the window still seals tight.

The big 413-ci engine may look original on the outside, but inside all has been renewed. Most of the original ancillary components were bolted back onto the block, and the valve covers, with their factory-applied Imperial decals still looking decent, were preserved instead of being repainted. A Mopar electronic ignition and 104-plus octane fuel additive keep the mighty engine purring at its optimal best.

Buick Buddies

Father and son team up to own a pair of Flint-built originals.

Y EARS AGO, WHEN SONS came of age to buy their first car, they always bought the same brand of car that their father drove. Rarely does it happen the other way around.

In this case, Ray Litwin's son, Matthew, was the first in the Litwin family to buy a Buick, an all-original Roadmaster sedan. A few years later, when they heard of a 1961 Invicta that was for sale nearby, the father and son duo went for a look-see. At the urging of Matt (who told Ray that if Ray didn't buy the car then he would instead), Ray decided that this original early 1960s sedan was too good to pass up.

Today, father and son are both members of the Buick Club of America, and travel to club meets and car shows together. And soon, when they're finished with the extension to Matt's garage, they will be working on Ray's 1956 Roadmaster alongside Matt's 1972 Skylark Custom convertible, all the while maintaining the originality of their two unrestored gems as best they can.

1952 Buick Roadmaster

Rare today is the young person who can truly appreciate big American cars of the early postwar era, and rarer still for them to understand the value and importance of maintaining an unrestored car's originality. One such enthusiast is Matthew Litwin, a 35-year-old associate editor at *Hemmings Motor News*, who's owned this well-preserved 1952 Buick Roadmaster four-door sedan since he bought it from a good friend back in 1996.

When Matthew first bought his Roadmaster, he said his original intention was to "keep it as is, other than required maintenance. At one point in time, I considered restoring the door upholstery and floor carpet. But after talking to Bill Hirsch one day at Hershey, it quickly occurred to me that a car is truly original only once. Hirsch also told me, being a young age, I should enjoy the car now, as is, because if I took the time to restore it I might be afraid to enjoy it—there's always time for restoration later in life when it's truly worn out and ready for it."

Withstanding the urge to tear the car apart and make it new again is easy to overcome, but replacing original parts because you have to is a lot harder than many people might think. It's a necessary evil that even Matthew finds difficult. "Resisting the temptation to replace semi-worn or torn items is the most difficult part of maintaining the car's originality. Mechanically, it's virtually impossible because the little bits will wear out and

break—it's all the other parts, both interior and exterior, that tell a story if you take the time to listen.

"I've always gone with the thought, 'you know what you have, and what's correct.' Unless you've restored the car yourself, it's really anyone's guess as to which parts were 'correct' during the process. You also lose a valuable time capsule and piece of history once it's been restored."

Some of those factory-installed components that had to be changed include the brakes shoes, brake master cylinder, and spark plugs; all four tires were replaced with bias-ply wide whitewalls. A heavy-duty Optima battery has supplanted the original battery for now, and soon, if need be, Matthew will be rebuilding the front end and the lever shocks to maintain the big Road-master's silky-smooth ride quality.

Like most old cars, when they were new they were used to meet the owner's daily transportation needs and this Buick was no different. Its battle scars include holes in the fabric that surround the door handles due to constant use, frayed edges on the carpet, and a singular hole in the driver's lower seat back. And what was once a light blue material on the bolster has now faded to a welcoming gray.

"The ability to get in it and go without worrying about a pebble putting a nick in the paint or hitting a rut in the road," is what Matthew likes best about his unrestored Roadmaster. "It's already had its parking-lot battles and survived mini highway missiles. I just have to make sure it starts every time and runs right. I also don't have to worry about friends and family climbing in and out of the spacious four-door."

Flaws and all, Matthew said that he will never part with his Buick. "It's been a big part of my life for so long, I'd give up my house first before selling the car. It has a spirit that's always willing to go the extra mile without any complaints, and loves to run. I've had it over 70 miles per hour and it had a lot more left! Besides, I always receive lots of compliments about its originality. Most everyone prefers to see the car as it really was in 1952."

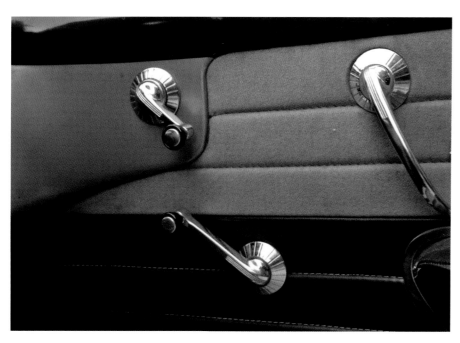

The soft blue mohair-type fabric and the multimaterial door panels have resisted more than a half-century of use, and the chrome-plated handles still shine like new. Once the tubes warm up, the sounds through the sizeable radio grille come through loud and clear.

Proving just how well engineered and ruggedly built Buick cars from the 1950s are, the 320.2-ci Fireball straight-eight engine has now traveled over 82,000 miles and it still runs as smoothly as ever. Smoother still is the Dynaflow automatic transmission—neither engine nor transmission has ever been apart, nor do they require any work.

On the trunk lid's ornate metal handle/lamp assembly the original red "Dyna" and "Flow" lenses were removed for safekeeping and replaced with reproduction lenses, much like the AC Heavy Duty Air Cleaner assembly, which has seen better days.

1961 Buick Invicta

Brustelon Buick in Mystic, Connecticut, had been home to this time capsule four-door Invicta since the car was initially delivered to them back in 1961. After it was finished being used as a "long-term demo" by the dealership's owner, and with 67,229 miles showing on the odometer, the car was placed in a heated barn, where it sat for many years, until it was put on display in the dealership's body shop showroom back in the summer of 2001.

According to its current owner, Raymond Litwin of Hebron, Connecticut, "What made this 1961 Invicta all the more unique is that the vehicle had never had a registered owner—I'm the first!—and it was a completely original vehicle, a true time capsule. This car had zero rust, a couple of minor blemishes, some thin paint in a couple of spots, and worn carpet, but otherwise was in very good condition. Best of all, it ran like a Swiss watch. It was a classic no-brainer; I'll keep this car forever, and then it will go to my son Matt.

"This car is incredibly comfortable, stable, and stylish. The 445-ci Wildcat V8 is very responsive, especially when you've got that 93 octane going through all four barrels of its Rochester Quadra-Jet carburetor. Unlike my 1956 Riviera, it's vintage, yet modern from a drivability perspective, very predictable and easily controlled, with fabulous brakes, and horsepower! True four-door hardtops are not a common sight these days. And most importantly, as I mentioned above, it's my first collector car. I can't envision ever parting with it.

"We've been to a lot of cruises and car shows with this car and are always pleasantly surprised at how many people appreciate the originality and beauty of this car. We get a lot of questions and compliments, especially when people see it has less than 70,000 miles on the odometer."

Unlike the very popular A-body Skylarks and Gran Sports, finding most exterior trim pieces for these four-door Invictas is extremely difficult because years ago few people ever considered such four-models worth preserving and restoring, so the demand was never there. As a result, Raymond has found it virtually impossible to locate the rear door reflectors, Invicta fender emblems, interior door trim, and just about any new-old-stock trim piece. "Mechanical components are easy to find, so that's not a problem, at least not yet," Raymond said. "However, I continue to slowly acquire new-old-stock parts, particularly trim pieces, whenever I can find them, so that if I ever had a need to replace a part I'll have it on hand."

Thankfully, good old General Motors' mechanical durability means that rarely are any mechanical parts needed. Other than the usual parts that wear, the only nonoriginal part on this Buick is the exhaust system. The carburetor required a rebuild, but at least it's the same carb that came on the car.

Beyond the unspoiled steering wheel with its perfect rim, emblem, and chrome plating, the speedometer, clock, courtesy lamps, and Sonomatic AM radio all function without any problems.

"Mechanically, this car is in excellent condition. It's obviously been very well maintained, but appearance-wise it's beginning to show minor signs of being 46 years old. The hardest thing to resist is the temptation to clean up the engine and engine compartment. Ditto for the front-seat-area carpeting, which obviously has seen a lot of foot traffic. As I spend more and more time attending *Hemmings* cruise nights, Hershey, and other collector-car events, it's very obvious that there aren't a lot of truly all-original antique cars out there, so I will try to preserve this car's originality as best I can."

Raymond was quite pragmatic in his beliefs as to why unrestored cars are more desirable than restored cars. "Now that I've been in the hobby for over eight years, and as much as I really appreciate seeing restored cars of any vintage, what appeals most to me about original/unrestored cars is that what you see is exactly (except for aging) what the car looked like when it rolled off the assembly line. The original trim didn't align perfectly, so why would you want to spend a ton of money to make it so? Also, because it is all original and somewhat showing its age, I could care less if we get caught in a rain shower at a show or cruise night. Enjoy the ride, dry it off when you get home, and enjoy a refreshing cold Budweiser when you're finished—how many owners of trailer queens do that?"

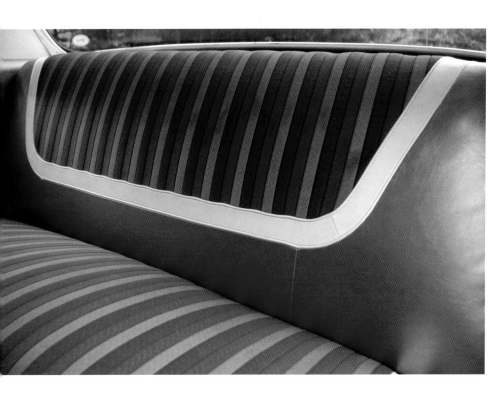

The vinyl material that Buick used for their interiors is extremely durable and hard wearing as evidenced by the door panels and bench seats, which still look as good as the day they were first made. Even the armrests are in perfect condition.

Replacement radiator and heater hoses may not look authentic, but the rest of the engine compartment is. Nothing has needed servicing aside from the carburetor, which required a thorough cleaning due to a build-up of sediment.

Amazing Monza

A 1962 Corvair Monza 900 that survived the wrath of 46-and-counting upstate New York winters.

Owners of Corvairs are incredibly passionate and enthusiastic about their little air-cooled Bowties. Perhaps that is why most possess more than one of these rear-engined mechanical marvels. Harold Bassett of Troy, New York, is no different. Besides his 1966 Monza convertible, Harold's favorite is this 1962 Monza coupe, a car that has withstood the test of time, and upstate New York's harsh winter climate, far better than most. Not only is the exterior paint all original, as is nearly all of the interior upholstery and door panels, but the two carburetors have never been apart. Its flat-six engine never needed any work during the 86,000 miles it has traveled through life. Of course the tires and battery have been replaced due to normal wear and tear, and so too were both front and rear bumpers due to several minor dents and scrapes, but not the generator. It still charges the battery well, just as Delco engineered it to.

The Roman Red exterior finish sports the same paint that the Chevrolet workers applied nearly 40 years ago,

save for a few dark spots here and there, which seems to be a fairly common occurrence among Corvairs built with this color during this time. One rarely seen feature on early Corvairs of 1960–1963 vintage is the maroon-colored fiber board material on the inside of the trunk lid; most cars no longer have it, and if they do it's usually in poor condition. Not this one. It looks practically brand new, as does all of the surrounding paint. Even the splatter paint throughout the trunk looks like it was applied yesterday, and in the engine compartment there are still traces of the black undercoating the Chevy workers sprayed on the firewall to help prevent engine noise from entering the cabin.

Besides its originality, Harold explains one of the main reasons why this Corvair is so special to him: "This is my first collector car, and it has taken me places I would have not gone if I didn't have it. But what I like most about it is all the love and attention it gets. Most often people can't, or won't, believe it's original."

It takes lots of care to maintain an unrestored car's originality, but Harold told us that the most difficult part of maintaining that originality is "not allowing yourself to get carried away when you start a repair project. They're only original once."

This Corvair's flat-six engine is so original, neither of the two carburetors has ever been removed. The AC spark plug stencil atop the metal air cleaner assembly is still legible, and most of the factory-applied black sound-deadening coating is still on the firewall.

Rarely seen on first-generation Corvairs is the insulation panel that was fitted to the underside of the front hood. This panel is not only in excellent condition but it still wears the original spare tire instruction paper sticker. And the original Kleer View windshield washer glass bottle is still with the car.

Looking like the day it was first stitched together, the rear seat shows almost no wear. The same for the door panels; their aluminum trim panels are practically perfect, as is the chrome finish on the handles for the locks and windows. The instrument panel shows nary a flaw, and the plastic rim of the steering wheel hasn't a crack in sight.

As happened to most red Corvairs that General Motors painted during the early 1960s, there are small dark red marks scattered here and there, but not enough to warrant a repaint. After all, why cover up a company's quality control? At least the stainless-steel wheel covers were extremely well made.

Studebaker Sensations

The world's best-preserved 1964 Avanti R1 keeps company alongside an equally authentic 1957 Golden Hawk.

IF YOU DON'T BELIEVE IT PAYS to join a car club just ask George Salzmann. All members of the Studebaker Driver's Club receive the club's bi-monthly magazine, *Turning Wheels*, and it was in that publication in 2006 that George found among the classified ads this incredibly original Avanti R1.

While I was in George's backyard in Union, New Jersey, viewing this unbelievable Avanti—a car so original it looked like it just rolled off the assembly line at the Studebaker factory in South Bend, Indiana—I asked him what makes this car so special. "There are several reasons why," George replied. "This is a rare Sears Allstate Studebaker promotion car. It was equipped from the factory with Sears Allstate tires and an Allstate battery. And the car is completely original, having been driven only 4,300 miles since new. And more than that, I think the Avanti is one of the most unique and beautifully designed automobiles ever built."

Besides its low mileage, the single most important attribute of this truly one-of-a-kind Avanti is that every single part on the car is the exact same part that was installed on it when it was assembled in the Studebaker factory. George said, "No parts have been replaced to my knowledge, other than the gas and oil filters. I can't tell you which Avanti parts are hard to find because I haven't had to look for any parts, so I really don't know."

Some of the factory original parts that are still on the car, and in outstanding condition no less, are the very same parts that most other unrestored original automobiles don't have. This includes all eight Champion spark plugs and ignition wires, the Puralator air filter element, all engine and engine compartment decals, hoses, clamps, and the entire exhaust system including the mufflers and tailpipes. In addition, not only are all four 6.70x15 Allstate Guardsman whitewalls the original tires that were placed on the wheels back at the factory but so too is the spare tire. In fact, the spare tire has never been used, its protective blue tint is still clearly visible on the thin white sidewall. As a result, the tire jack has never been used either. And inside the glove box resides the original owner's manual and dealer service records.

To help preserve the car's originality, this Avanti has been garaged in a heated storage facility since it rolled off the Studebaker assembly line. The engine oil has been changed to Mobil One 10W-30 synthetic, and the old brake fluid was drained and replaced with Dot-5 synthetic. All the fluids are changed regularly regardless how few miles the car has been driven and only high-octane gas with a lead additive mixed in is used to power the 289-ci V8 engine.

The exterior chrome is perfect as well, and the factory-applied Avanti Red paint remains in excellent condition, wearing a deep shine as if it was just applied. The black vinyl upholstery is perfect with not a single wear mark evident anywhere. From the beauty vanity to the dashboard instruments and switches to the woodgrain appliqué on the console, every square inch of this car is flawless. As one would expect from such a rarely used specimen, none of the screws, bolts, or nuts have ever been touched with a screwdriver or a socket since the day they were fastened down all those years ago. In simple terms, this is a rolling artifact, a window into the world of Avanti production circa 1963–64.

Although he only takes the Avanti out four or five times a year, rarely adding more than 50 miles annually to the barely broken-in odometer, when George does get the urge to do some serious Studebaker motoring he takes out his other South Bend beauty, a 1957 Golden Hawk. This too is an all-original, unrestored Studebaker. Apart from the tires, battery, filters, exhaust system, and carpeting, nothing else has ever been replaced. From the heater and radiator hoses to the wide belt that drives the supercharger, all else is original to this car.

The gold and white paint has several character flaws, but nothing serious, just the usual minor chips and scratches. Most three-year-old cars don't even look this good. Same goes for the interior, it's in very good condition; clean and wear-free. Yet George has driven it to

No, it's not a restored engine compartment. It's what an Avanti's engine looks like when it's been driven less than 4,500 miles from when it was new. The "4162" inspection mark is still on the underside of the hood, the Prestolite regulator appears as if it has just been taken out of a box, and every single factory-applied decal and sticker is present and accounted for.

several Studebaker events, the farthest was a Studebaker Driver's Club International Meet that was held in Wisconsin several years ago. "We put over 2,500 miles on it during that roundtrip drive, and it drove like a top. Perfectly smooth and trouble free."

"I think unrestored, original cars are more desirable because you can see how well the car has been maintained and cared for over the years. Also, you can tell if the car has been damaged due to an accident or weather-related problems."

The condition of the Avanti's interior is simply astonishing; it's better than perfect. The wood appliqué on the dashboard and console is flawless as is every single gauge, switch, and inch of chrome trim; even the doorjambs are unblemished. Truly a one-of-a-kind example of fine Studebaker workmanship.

Now this is amazing. The original Allstate spare tire has never been used nor has the protective blue coating on the whitewall been removed. Even the plywood cover with the jacking instructions still stuck to its underside is in excellent condition.

Studebaker Golden Hawk

Not only is this 289-ci Studebaker V8 all original and completely untouched, but so too are its super-charger belt, radiator hoses, and Delco-Remy generator.

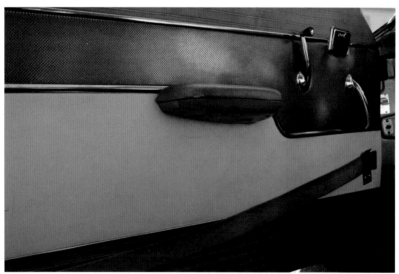

It may look brand new but it's not; just a carefully well-maintained interior. The golden and white seat vinyl has not a single split, the decorative metal panels shine like new, and the engine-turned dashboard has that just-installed appearance. The same goes for all the gauges, headliner, and steering wheel.

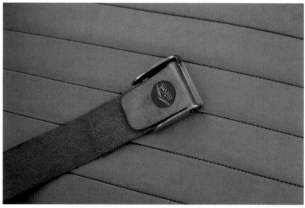

The interior of this Golden Hawk features two rarely seen original items: seatbelts with the Studebaker-Packard S-P sticker and the "Studebaker Craftsmanship With A Flair" emblems that are affixed to the front seats.

Childhood Connection

The well-preserved nature of this 1965 Ford Fairlane provides well-preserved memories for its owner.

"THE FACT THAT IT WAS UNTOUCHED and belonged to someone I knew," is the main reason why this plain Jane four-door Fairlane sedan is so special, says owner John Rich of Sushan, New York. "It was owned by a man I knew from childhood. He ran the local ice cream shop, Jacko's, and he only drove it on Sunday afternoons to take his wife for a ride. That is why my intentions with this car, since the day I bought it from his son back in 1993, have always been to keep it local and preserve it."

John is the consummate old-car enthusiast. Besides this original Fairlane, he owns a 1903 Stevens-Duryea, 1918 Detroit Electric, 1934 Auburn Phaeton convertible sedan, a Willys-Knight touring car that he's currently restoring, 1923 Citroen, several flathead Fords, a Volvo 122, and a bunch of pickup trucks including a 1937 Graham Brothers. Old farming equipment makes up a substantial part of John's 75-vehicle-strong collection, including several tractors, such as his beloved 1938 Allis-Chalmers and a very rare front-wheel-drive 1936 Massey-Harris. And let's not forget the 1916 Kelsey prototype awaiting restoration. Perhaps that is why this Fairlane only gets driven some 100 miles per year.

Since day one, this Fairlane has been well cared for and stored safely inside, away from the harsh elements of upstate New York. Today it resides in an insulated barn alongside all of John's other vehicles. Due to such care and limited use, the back seat looks as if it has never been sat in; the ashtrays were never used. Everything in the interior, including every square inch of the red vinyl and cloth upholstery, is in excellent condition.

The only major component that's worn and soon to be replaced is the clutch, which seems odd because this column-shifted three-speed car has been driven just 19,000 miles since new. The tires, battery, oil, and air filter have been replaced, but that's it. In fact, the little 200-ci straight-six engine purrs as smoothly as the day it was first assembled.

The white exterior paint has lost a little of its shine and there are a few minor chips and scratches, but all of the paint is original, as is all the exterior chrome trim, weather stripping, and glass. Throughout the body and engine compartment there are several yellow "PAINT OK" and dated inspection markings that the Ford workers stamped on the car when their jobs were complete; every stamp looks like it was applied yesterday.

While some car collectors appreciate original classic cars simply because they are rare, John takes a more realistic view regarding his Fairlane's originality. "Being unrestored, it shows that the car was not perfect even when new."

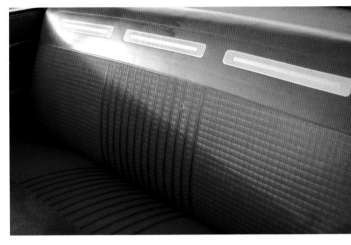

Aside from the worn-off paint above the ignition switch, the interior is virtually brand new. The door panels may be a little dirty but they're perfect, as is the armrest. And the rear seats were hardly ever sat upon.

The standard straight-six engine of 200 cubic inches has never needed any internal work. Everything on it is a factory-original part, including the spark plug wires, distributor cap, starter, and alternator. The air cleaner still hosts the factory-applied "AUTOLITE SPARK PLUGS" decals.

Original factory details and period information abound on this base-model Fairlane sedan, such as the stenciled yellow lettering codes that appear on both sides of the radiator support. The oil change stickers show that a 10-30 oil change took place on 4/16/82 when there were 15,808 miles on the car. The odometer still has not reached 20,000 miles.

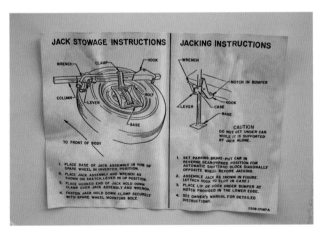

The factory spare tire has been used but the original jack above is practically new. The floor mat is in decent shape and the new-looking jacking instructions have yellowed with age.

Love Thy Neighbor

A few good deeds was all it took for one car enthusiast to be presented with this incredible 1967 Cadillac Eldorado.

IT'S ALWAYS A GOOD THING to be nice to your neighbors, especially the older citizens who could use some help around their house. Once in a while, when you least expect it, they'll reward you with something very special. Like a car.

"This Cadillac was a gift from my New Jersey neighbor, and what a gift it was," Joseph Giolito of Manchester, Vermont, told me when I met him one evening during one of the *Hemmings* summer cruise nights. "It's all original, and had been driven only 43,000 miles. The back seat and trunk were never used, and it still has the original spare tire in place."

Joe's generous neighbor was an elderly lady who was no longer able to drive. She wanted to see the Eldorado she bought back in 1967 go to someone who would appreciate it as much as she did during the 37 years that she owned it. She chose the perfect person, because Joe promised her that he'd take good care of it and never sell it.

Finished in a pleasant-looking light metallic green exterior with a black vinyl roof, the inviting interior was ordered in a vinyl and cloth combination in a matching green. According to Joe, "The interior is in #1 condition, not worn, and very clean. It even has the original

floor mats, which still look new. It was owned by a single person, so there is no wear or tear on anything. However, I did have to replace the accessory belts and the tires. And because the radiator was clogged with silt, it also had to be replaced; fortunately, these are not rare. Thankfully, nothing else is needed. Absolutely nothing."

So how does Joe maintain the car's originality? "It must be kept in climate-controlled storage," Joe said. "The original paint is 41 years old and must be kept cleaned and waxed and all the rubber parts must be treated regularly so they don't dry out. It's not a daily-driver type of car; I drive it about 700 miles every year. Most of that mileage is put on when I'm driving it to various local car shows and when I attend the *Hemmings* cruise nights during the summer. I mainly keep it garaged with a cover on it."

Besides the car's well-kept state, Joe said this about his Cadillac: "It was an innovative personal luxury coupe that oozed style, and that was unheard of back in the 1960s. The Eldorado remains one of the most imaginative cars produced during that decade—it really is one of a kind."

Unlike other Cadillacs from this era that have been crashed, dented, and repainted; that had to have their engines and transmissions either rebuilt or replaced; or that needed new suspension and brake systems installed, this Eldorado is a truly original specimen. And Joe appreciates that fact. "They're only original once. I really like the attention it gets when I take it to car

shows; people can't believe that nothing had ever been done to the car except replace the tires," says Joe. "As it gets older it gets more and more attention, and has been photographed and written about by many car enthusiasts. Most particularly, it feels great to have an original collector car. I have lots of fun telling the whole story—how it was a gift. I still can't believe it. I never had such a great gift."

With only 48,000 miles on the car today, the big 429-ci V8 engine and automatic transmission are hardly broken in. The entire powertrain runs ultra smoothly, with nary a hint of noises or vibrations. And the rarely seen orange Non-Vented FC 46 oil filler cap is still in place, as is the radiator cap warning sticker.

One of the most amazing aspects of this sleekly styled Eldorado is that everything still works, including all the door courtesy lamps, glove box lamp, and ignition buzzer. And all the upholstery, floor mats, steering wheel, and the entire dashboard are in showroom-new condition. It's a real time capsule, and an incredibly well-preserved one at that.

Aside from a few worn spots and a minor rock chip or two, the entire body remains covered in the same paint that Cadillac sprayed on more than 40 years ago, and it still shines up nicely. All the badges and trim have remained free of pitting, and both bumpers have retained that brand-new appearance; even the taillamp lenses haven't faded. That's Cadillac quality the way it used to be.

Bonded for Life

Boyhood dream comes true via a newspaper ad for this 1974 Dodge Charger.

"TILL DEATH DO US PART. I'll never sell it." That's how strongly committed Andrew Vourlos, of Smithtown, Long Island, is to his all-original vintage 1974 Dodge Charger. Since he was a kid, Andrew has been a huge fan of Richard Petty, and has always been passionate about Petty's number 43 Charger that he raced in the early 1970s. So it was no coincidence that Andrew ended up owning the very same model Mopar that he has been lusting after for some 25 years.

Andrew spotted the car listed for sale in his local newspaper, *Newsday*, in 1998. The asking price was $5,000, but Andrew ended up getting the car for half that amount once the elderly lady—the car's original owner—learned that he wouldn't modify the Charger in any way. It was her late husband's car, and she wanted it to go to a good home, so Andrew got the nod among several other potential buyers.

"When I first saw the car sitting in her driveway, I couldn't believe the straightness of the body," Andrew remembered. "I got down on my knee and carefully looked for signs of rust on the quarter panels, but couldn't find any. I looked underneath to see if there was rust on the floorboards and inner fenders, but to my astonishment, there was none. In my mind, I was saying,

'Can this really be an original Chrysler product from the 19970s with no rust?'

"I always wanted a Charger, and to find one in such original condition was like a gift from God. It doesn't matter in the least to me that it's not a 'muscle' version; it is just fine and gives me all the enjoyment I could want. It only had 27,000 miles on it in 1998, so for me it was almost like buying a brand-new 1974 Dodge Charger."

Besides the Charger's well-preserved underside, the body was in equally fine condition. All the body panels were original to the car, and the factory-applied Dark Moonstone metallic paint still held a decent shine, and still does today. Even the black vinyl roof shows no signs of aging. The weather stripping, chrome trim, and glass are original, and all are in very good condition. This is especially true of the Lucerne Blue vinyl interior and dash; there isn't a rip or crack in sight. A truly well-preserved Mopar of the highest order.

With 39,800 miles now showing on the odometer, the Dodge had been used sparingly and had always been garaged and well maintained. "All the mechanical parts on its 318-ci V8 are original," Andrew proudly stated. This includes the starter, alternator, radiator, ignition coil, wheel bearings, universal joints, TorqueFlite transmission, and the 2.71-geared differential. "Every now and then, the number-five cylinder will have a lifter that sticks before it pumps up with oil, but that's it." The only part

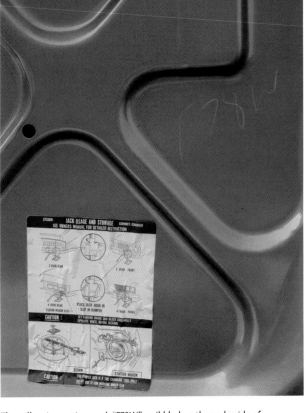

Thanks to the original owners who always kept the Charger garaged, the Dark Moonstone metallic paint has been extremely well preserved. A twice-yearly polish and waxing ensure that it will last. And the black vinyl roof appears as if it had just been glued down, it's that perfect.

The yellow inspection mark "F78W" scribbled on the underside of the trunk lid probably meant the size of the whitewall tire that the car was to be fitted with. The spare tire is original to this Charger, and so too are the headlamps. In fact, the rear brake shoes and drums are original as well, as are both front brake rotors.

that had to be rebuilt was the master brake cylinder, and the accelerator pump on the original two-barrel Carter carburetor was replaced. New shocks and mufflers were replaced, too.

"The first time I got under the car, I noticed that there was almost no paint on the bottoms of the rocker panels! Irregular gaps where body panels meet are noticeable, and fit and finish are not going to win any assembly awards. The factory-paint pinstripe that was standard on hardtop models is wavy, and the thickness is not consistent."

Although he replaced the original dry-rotted tires with correctly sized 215/70R14 BFGoodrich Radial T/As, Andrew resisted the temptation to upgrade to larger 15-inch tires on the more sporting Rally or Magnum 500 wheels. "Granted, these would look better, but I wanted to preserve as much originality as possible. In fact, the right-side rims still have the Lynch Road assembly-line chalk marks on them," Andrew said. "So, the deluxe wheel covers and stock tire size will remain for now.

"The first year I owned it, I put about 5,000 miles on it during the summer and changed the oil three times to make sure it was purged of the old oil that had resided

in the crankcase from the previous owner. Now I only drive it about 1,500 miles a year, mainly to cruise nights in the summer and the occasional car show. In traffic, it's big, it's nerve-wracking. There's no passenger-side door mirror and there's a blind spot along the quarter panel, so lane changes are a little hard. I'm paranoid about driving it on Long Island's crowded roads, so on Sunday drives I take it out early, before the crowds come out. I change the oil and filter every spring and make sure the tires are properly inflated. It's a pleasure car that I intend on keeping original forever so that future generations can see an example of 1970s Americana."

When I asked Andrew why he thinks original cars are more desirable than restored cars, his reply was quite inspiring: "Cars, like people, are time travelers, and an original car is like an old veteran. You walk up to it, greet it, and admire it for the conditions that it weathered as it went through its life. Every piece, every aspect, is a reflection of the past, being viewed in the present. You can't help but stand there in awe and be reminded of what roads it traveled, what sights it has seen. It humbles me, and makes me feel wonderful."

Inside, the attractive Lucerne Blue vinyl upholstery, door panels, and dashtop are in remarkable condition for their age, with nary a crack or rip in sight. Even the carpeting is original to the car, as are the floor mats.

All that Andrew's done to the engine is replace the dried-out valve cover gaskets to stop the oil leaks, and he repainted the valve covers in the original blue paint. Even the orange ignition wires are the original date-coded wires that were fitted to the engine when it was new. All the factory-applied stickers and decals still exist.

A Working Man's Collection

Just down the road from the headquarters of General Electric, this Schenectady, New York, garage is home to one man's collection of unrestored drivers.

With original Chevrolet dealer showroom banners—circa 1950 and 1954—hanging from the overhead steel trusses, thus lending the garage a comforting feeling of being back in the safe, carefree days of the Eisenhower administration, every car and truck you see here runs and drives with just the twist of its key.

FADED PAINT, TARNISHED CHROME, stained upholstery, and delaminated glass. These are just some of the many positive attributes that owner Tom Nicchi loves about the condition of his cars and trucks.

The collection spans about 40 vehicles, all of which, aside from 1957 and 1960 Thunderbirds and a lone 1975 Triumph TR6, have been built by General Motors. Half of the collection is made up of half-ton GMC and Chevy pickup trucks and a pair of one-ton sedan deliveries; the other half focuses mostly on early postwar two-door sedans. Apart from a pair of Buicks and a couple of Cadillac convertibles, Chevrolet cars are what Tom appreciates the most. Most important, none have been restored.

"I will never own, nor do I want to own, a restored car. It just doesn't make any sense to me," Tom said with conviction in his voice. "If I owned a car that had been restored, especially one that was done to concours condition, I would be afraid to drive it. I would be worrying about it all the time. How much fun is that?"

Looking over Tom's array of cars, with their scratched paint, touched-up exteriors, dirty tires, and interiors that are in desperate need of some serious elbow grease, I got the feeling that this is one sincere old-car enthusiast who really does appreciate his cars for what they are, not what they can be made to look like.

"Every car you see here runs. Go ahead, point to a car and I'll start it," Tom said to me. So I chose the blue 1946 Chevy. He then made his way to the driver's-side window, reached in, and turned the key. "I told you it would start. They all will start," Tom said with this huge smile on his face. "Keeping them off the road while they're being restored is a waste of time. I'd rather be driving them and having fun. I like their originality. So what if they're not perfect? I'd much rather own original unrestored cars that need work that I can drive everyday than cars that have to be trailered. That is what owning old cars should be all about."

The red 1952 Chevrolet was repainted years ago but the engine, drivetrain, and suspension are just as GM built them. The blue 1946 Chevrolet Stylemaster still has its factory-applied blue paint, although the paint on the front fender has worn down to the primer. Tom plans on keeping its originality in check by preserving what's left of the factory finish. Everything else on this car is original, too.

This trio of 1937 Chevrolet sedans are regularly used for local weddings, and when Tom feels like driving around Albany in something completely different from what's around him. One car has been repainted but the other two are mostly original; all are powered by their original flathead engines and manual transmissions.

Trucks are dear to Tom's heart, especially the Advanced Design series from General Motors. This particular 1948 GMC half-ton pickup still wears its original green paint—or whatever's left of it—proudly. Tom has no desire to repaint the truck because he enjoys driving it just the way it is.

Touched up here and there, this unrestored 1949 Chevrolet Fleetmaster has been fitted with radial tires. Tom says that since he put on the radials the car drives far better and steers more accurately; its handling and braking ability have improved too. This makes him feel more comfortable when he's driving in traffic.

HPOF

The AACA's Historical Preservation
of Original Features class.

All the way from Nowata, Oklahoma, Connie Moore brought his very rare 1970 Ford Ranchero. The original black paint is in better condition than most cars half its age, and the yellow/orange/red fade stripe was in equally fine shape. Even the susceptible cargo bed showed very little use.

Alan Blay, a well-known collector-car insurance agent from Merrick, Long Island, and a recognized expert on early Corvettes, brought his mostly original 1957 Corvette for HPOF certification. Although the seats have been reupholstered, the rest of the interior, like the exterior paint and trim, is original to the car. Parked alongside was a well-worn yet still mostly original 1949 Ford coupe that makes a good reference guide for other enthusiasts restoring the same model. The nicely preserved 1967 Plymouth GTX alongside it is also a very good representative of its breed, proving that even muscle cars survived the test of time—and racing—so well.

THE LEADING NATIONAL CLUB dedicated to the preservation of collector cars is the AACA. Based in Hershey, Pennsylvania, and whose local region is responsible for hosting the world's largest collector-car swap meet and car show each October, the AACA ensures that original, unrestored cars are properly documented on a national level.

As listed in the AACA's Official Judging Manual rulebook: "Since its founding, the AACA has been dedicated to the preservation, restoration and maintenance of vehicles. In the furtherance of the 'preservation' mission, the AACA Board of Directors in 1987 established a program to encourage the saving and display of collector vehicles in their original, as-manufactured condition. The Historical Preservation of Original Features program encourages owners of vehicles 35-years-old and older, retaining significant original features, to allow them to remain in this original condition, and to show them at National Meets. A vehicle may be entirely 'original' or it may have certain 'original' features such as paint, chassis, upholstery, engine compartment, etc, that are essentially as delivered. These vehicles will not be point judged. They will be certified using a percentage system which includes a total average percentage of the original features of the exterior, interior, chassis, and engine. The vehicle must receive a score of sixty-five (65%) percent or above to receive certification. They will be recognized at the awards ceremony and will receive an exhibition award. A certification plaque will be presented to each vehicle upon acceptance into the Historical Preservation of Original Features (HPOF) category. Vehicles entering the HPOF category will be prohibited from future registration in any other competition or exhibition class. If the vehicle is restored, certification in HPOF category will be voided. No previous National First Prize winners are accepted. An HPOF certified vehicle that is significantly restored will lose its HPOF certification. HPOF certification remains with the vehicle even if there is a change of ownership."

As you can see by the above well thought-out guidelines, the AACA looks at the preservation of old cars, trucks, and motorcycles in a pretty serious manner. Their rules are strict and the judging of their members' cars quite rigorous, but it's all done to ensure that original, properly preserved vehicles are given the honor and recognition that they rightfully deserve.

To view firsthand many of these rare and outstanding unrestored automobiles, all you have to do is attend one of the many AACA meets held each year throughout the country. There you will be amazed at not only the extraordinary originality of the cars on display but also the rarity of some of the vehicles entered in the HPOF category.

The cars shown here were photographed at the 2007 Eastern Division National Fall Meet—known the world over simply as "Hershey." Several of the cars shown were not on display in the HPOF class but instead were in the Hershey car corral, where it's not unusual to find more than two dozen truly outstanding, low-mileage, original cars, and sometimes a few trucks, presented for sale.

At the regional meets there are usually between 40 or 60 cars, depending on where the meet is held, entered in the HPOF category, but in October at Hershey it's not unusual to see well over 100 original vehicles vying for their HPOF certification. It really is a spectacular sight to see all these wonderful unrestored collector cars on the show field.

For more information on the AACA and its important HPOF category, visit their Web site: www.aaca.org. Better yet, join the club, and be a part of this 50,000-member-strong organization that is the backbone of the collector-car hobby.

One of the most popular cars in the 2007 HPOF class was this unrestored 1956 Corvette belonging to George Hughes Jr. from Springfield, Pennsylvania. There were crowds inspecting this solid-axle beauty throughout the day, all marveling at its original features and factory details.

It may not have been a high-performance 427 model. Still, this 289-powered 1966 Ford four-door sedan had only accumulated 15,000 miles since it was first built. The original burgundy paint was in excellent condition, the upholstery was perfect, and all the chrome trim was tarnish free.

There are many truly great deals to be had over in the Hershey car corral, such as this incredible 1954 Ford two-door sedan. The sign read "All Original, 3,000 Miles From New, You Need To Look." The paint was just as Ford sprayed it, a little flat and not so smooth, but it's that kind of originality that's so appealing to serious enthusiasts.

Long, wide, and exceptionally authentic, the placard in the window of this 1966 Chrysler Imperial stated: "Original Car, 20,390 Miles." From its exterior paint and blue interior to its lavish grille and chrome trim, every portion of this well-appointed Chrysler was in above-average condition.

Chapter 5

Unbridled Power: Completely Original Muscle Cars

The one type of car that is probably harder to find in completely original condition than any other collector car, regardless of age or rarity, is muscle cars. With their high-performance engines and stout drivetrains, these machines were built to race. And that's exactly what most of them did.

Be it the street or the strip, muscle cars were engineered, bred, and modified for heads-up competition. Many crashed, and others were just left to rot away outdoors once the gas crisis hit, while most were used as everyday transport.

This is why there are so few original muscle cars remaining, thus it's a real treat to see one that has been well taken care of without having had any modifications or crash-damaged repairs done to it. And to discover one that is still clothed in its original paint—with paint that still looks new—is a remarkable find indeed.

Everyone has a memorable story about owning, racing or wanting a muscle car, but to find one today that has remained exactly as its Detroit manufacturer built it is indeed an extraordinary discovery.

Stashed-Away Solid Axle

*Not just any 1960 Corvette, but a
dual-quad original.*

JUST WHEN YOU THINK all the good collector cars have
been found, one comes up for sale right in your very
own backyard. And, if you're lucky, it could be a fairly
rare car at that. Such is the story of this solid-axle
Corvette, one of 2,364 built with the 270-horsepower
dual-quad engine option.

For 33 years this car was stored in a garage with 20
other cars of interest, one of which is a Plymouth
Superbird that is still there. Its elderly owner refused to
part with it even after she was offered a handsome six-fig-
ure sum for it. This same owner didn't want to sell the
Corvette, either, but finally decided to let it go. Robert Tri-
antafillos, a machinist from Oxford, Connecticut, heard
of the car through a friend, and was amazed that it was
located less than two miles from his Connecticut home.

"It took nine hours to clear a path just to get it out,"
Robert remembers about the day he went to retrieve this
Ermine-white Corvette with the Sateen silver coves.
"While it sat unused, mice ruined the interior and con-
vertible top, but the paint was about as you see it.

"I've always had a soft spot for Corvettes," Robert ad-
mitted. "I sold an original one years ago and regretted
it ever since." Besides this 1960 model, Robert is currently building a 1954 Corvette modern-day hot rod
that's powered by an LS1 V8, complete with fuel injec-

tion. Also scattered about the basement of his house
and in the barn is a 1966 Sting Ray coupe that will be restored after the 1954 is completed.

"Most used Corvettes are disappointing," Robert said.
"When you get them home and start looking closely at
them, you'll see all sorts of undetected problems, body
or chassis damage, poor repairs, missing parts, and
poorly done modifications. But this car turned out to be
much better, and that's because it was well cared for by
the last owner. This particular Corvette may not shine
like a restored car but it runs great, and always draws a
crowd. Best of all, it's a great driver."

Driving the car for more than 80,000 miles back in the
day then letting it sit in an unheated barn without proper
protection for more than three decades was not very
kind to many of the car's mechanical components. As
a result, the original 283-ci V8 engine had to be rebuilt,
along with both carburetors. Thankfully, these are the
car's original carbs: Carter four-barrel WCFBs.

The entire brake system also had to be rebuilt, which
included new hoses, lines, wheel cylinders, and shoes.
The fuel system too needed replacement: a new gas
tank, hoses, lines, pump, and filter had to replace the
originals because everything was either clogged or
rusted. Even the original radiator was in poor condition,
but instead of staying with a correct-looking Harrison
unit, Robert decided to upgrade the cooling system with
a Griffin aluminum radiator. This allows him to take the

car on long drives, which he and his wife do often, without fear of overheating.

One of Robert's biggest goals is to find a set of useable, original seat covers and carpeting to replace the reproductions he was forced to install due to the mice damage. But that's it. He plans on keeping the body just the way it is, saying that he doesn't have to worry about damaging the paint when he's out driving it or when it's parked at a car show or cruise night.

To date, the odometer shows 88,500 miles; however, with each passing year another 1,500 miles are added. "We use it all the time," Robert said. "My wife, Nancy, and I will continue having fun with this car for a long time. She likes it as much as I do. Raindrops don't scare us.

"Most people prefer a nicely restored car, but anybody can restore or buy a shiny restored car. What I like most about original cars is that they stand out in a crowd. And, of course, that they are getting hard to find. Most important, because their quality differs from car to car, they should be preserved as a benchmark for cars that are being restored."

Its factory paint covered with battle scars, there's no second-guessing this Corvette's originality. From its chipped paint, exposed fiberglass, and tarnished trim, being stored in a New England barn for more than three decades did this car absolutely no good. But it's perhaps one of the most honest-looking solid-axle models that you will ever find.

Cleaned and rebuilt without being overrestored, the original 283-ci V8 still retains all the ancillary components that it was first built with, including both four-barrel Carter WCFB carburetors. The original black paint remaining on the hood locks proves the St. Louis factory workers painted them in suit.

Showing years of enjoyable use, the telltale scratches on the painted dashboard are a gentle reminder that this car was driven regularly before being stored away. The radio is missing, but all else, including the shifter floor plate and the clock panel, is there and in very good condition.

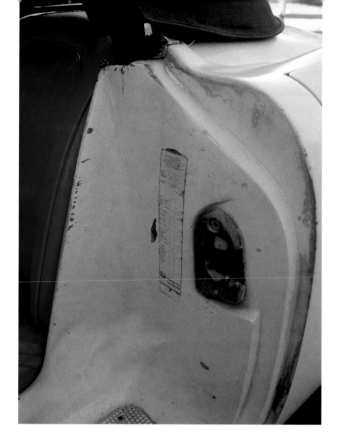

The paint on the driver's-side doorjamb has been rubbed down to the factory gray primer. The information on the original oil change sticker has faded, but the Champion Spark Plug sticker shows that plugs were changed at 58,000 miles.

CAUTION

THIS VEHICLE EQUIPPED WITH LIMITED SLIP DIFFERENTIAL. REAR WHEEL MAY DRIVE IF IN CONTACT WITH GROUND EVEN THOUGH OPPOSITE WHEEL IS RAISED. DO NOT RUN ENGINE WITH VEHICLE ON JACK UNLESS TRANS-MISSION IS IN NEUTRAL OR PARK. SEE OWNER'S MANUAL.

PRINTED IN U.S.A.   7-22-58   PART NO. 3746

Well worn but incredibly original, the trunk provides Corvette histori-ans with the proper knowledge of the way the factory really finished them. The wooded spare tire cover is still solid and the warning sticker about the limited-slip differential is a desirable piece of paperwork.

Masked Muscle

A 1965 Ford Galaxie 500 LTD that's a genuine dual-quad muscle machine.

THE TOWN OF BENNINGTON, VERMONT, comes alive every other Thursday night throughout the summer when *Hemmings Motor News* hosts a cruise night. The parking lot behind the *Hemmings* Sunoco filling station is usually jammed full of American collector cars, European sports cars, well-restored muscle cars, interesting street rods, and several desirable classics including one well-running Stanley Steamer. And parked silently among all these wonderful old cars is perhaps the rarest car of them all, yet practically everyone in attendance walks past it, thinking it's just some local old man's well-worn Galaxie. But oh how mistaken they are: This old "family car" is anything but just another old Ford.

Lars Severance, a *Hemmings* cruise night regular and owner of this incredible muscle machine, knows all too well just how special his car is. "The best thing I like about my Galaxie," he says, "is its rarity. Most people walk past it not realizing its rarity and originality. Full-size Ford muscle is obscure compared to Road Runners and GTOs. In fact, there are only two 427 LTDs of 1965 vintage known to have survived. It's also extremely unusual to see a high-performance muscle car that also has a lot of luxury options. Usually the buyer who wanted maximum performance was also seeking minimum weight. And it's this very engine that makes the

car so special to me. The 427 is the most famous engine in the history of Ford racing. The Galaxie 427 competed successfully in both the NHR and NASCAR back in the mid-1960s."

This particular Galaxie 500 has the optional LTD trim package, and those incredibly rare glass headlamp covers. Its Caspian Blue exterior paint and blue vinyl roof are both factory original, as is the dark blue cloth upholstery and headliner. Under the hood rests a massively powerful 427-ci V8. With its dual-quad Holley carburetor setup and low-riser "wedge" cylinder heads that squeeze the air-fuel mixture with a high 11.1:1 compression ratio, according to Ford's specifications, it produces a very healthy—and conservative—425 horsepower and 480 lbs.ft of torque. A Top Loader four-speed assists with the transfer of power to the rear.

Of course, there is a downside to owning a full-size muscle car like this Galaxie. As Lars put it, "Because Ford Galaxies have a small following, reproduction and replacement parts are more difficult to find. Some of the high-performance parts are also harder to find."

Yet, like any old car that's more than 40 years old, especially one like this fabulous Ford that is used regularly throughout Vermont's short yet glorious driving season, there comes a point where many of the wearing parts must be replaced. So through the years, Lars has had to replace the wheels, tires, fuel tank, exhaust system, brake hoses, and brake shoes. And to make the interior

The entire dual-quad Holley carburetor setup has been rebuilt, the intake beadblasted to look new, the "wedge" cylinder heads recut, and the special exhaust manifolds refinished—all are original parts to this numbers-matching 425-horsepower 427-ci V8. Most everything else is original, too, including the starter solenoid and all of its wiring.

a little more comfortable, the old worn and torn carpeting was replaced with a factory-correct reproduction set. Thankfully, all the really rare components that make this Galaxie so distinctive are still with the car. They include the factory exhaust headers, transistorized ignition, trunk-mounted reverb radio unit, and the aforementioned glass headlamp covers.

"I might like to have new seat covers made out of new-old-stock cloth," Lars said. "The car is original, and I know it's only original once, but I'm still on the fence because it is so solid; it would be a real easy restoration because it's solid like my '62 Galaxie G-code 406 hardtop. But I just don't know. Maybe I'll restore it one day, but it might be a long, long time.

"Although my car is mostly unrestored," says Lars, "it isn't nicely preserved as many others I have seen from the same time period. But it is a unique car to drive and enjoy. It's a beast, and it's really loud. At highway speed, when you have the windows rolled up, you can't hear the radio."

Factory Ford period-correct headlamp covers are made of glass and are extremely rare. The 427 emblems on the lower front fenders showcase that this Fairlane is one of only two 427 LTDs known to exist. Vintage Vermont plates give it that period look.

An old set of SW gauges complement the stock four-speed shifter. The rest of the interior is completely original, including the padded dash and factory optional AM/FM radio with trunk-mounted reverb unit, although the carpet has been replaced. The front seats need to be reupholstered, but at least the rear seats and door panels don't have to be touched.

The vinyl roof and all its trimmings have held up well to the elements; in fact, they still retain a factory-fresh appearance. Inside the trunk the always-discarded cardboard panels that protect the quarter panel from getting dinged remain in excellent condition.

Shelby Sensation

The most original 1967 Shelby Mustang GT500 on the planet was found inside a remote barn in the North Carolina hills.

AFTER READING ABOUT this sensational find in Tom Cotter's latest book, *Hemi in the Barn*, I couldn't wait to view this Shelby up close when I learned that it was going to be on display at the nearby Saratoga Automobile Museum. On the first free Saturday available I headed over to Saratoga Springs, New York, to inspect this authentic muscle machine.

Inside the museum, sitting among upscale, unrestored classics including Lincoln, Packard, and Horch, this green Shelby stood out like a spotlit star on a Broadway stage. Like a magnet, it immediately drew me in, its untouched originality clearly evident from across the expansive room.

The environment inside the North Carolina barn hadn't been kind to the Mustang's metal, especially to its paint. Small chips, large chips, and sizeable sections worn down to the bare metal were everywhere. The chrome was peeling off the bumpers, and a triangular-shaped clothes hanger stood where the antenna once did. And those ever desirable 10-spoke Shelby mags were completely oxidized. If ever a car had character, this was it.

"It is totally unmolested, driven only by a woman," Tom said of his Shelby, which he co-owns with his friend, Jim Maxwell. "The car was literally parked in 1980 and hadn't been driven since. From the first moment it came into my possession my intention was to leave it as is." Although driven just 34,000 miles since new, and even though this irreplaceable artifact is one of very few completely authentic Shelby Mustangs known to exist, Tom and Jim decided back in 2006 to bring it to the Shelby American Automobile Club's national convention held that year at Virginia International Raceway. There, everyone marveled at its originality, but it was especially significant to owners of other 1967 Shelbys because it was the ultimate example to assist them in restoring their cars to previous unknown exacting, factory-correct, standards. According to Tom, "It was the hit of the SAAC meet at VIR when every judge in the place dropped what they were doing to spend an hour inspecting the most original car on the property."

"The steering wheel and horn button, which are very rare, are still on this car. So, too, is the original spare tire, and I have two additional original Goodyear Power Cushion tires. Reluctantly, we replaced the ignition points because, after 40 years, they were so badly burned—the original ones are in the trunk. As for the body, I thought once about having the car partially painted, but it won't happen. The paint and body will remain the same as long as we own it."

While keeping the car "as is" is the right thing to do, the negative aspect of doing so comes to light when showing the car in public because many, many people—

car enthusiasts included—just don't understand the intrinsic value of cars like this. "Having to put up with a bunch of clowns who ask, 'So, are you going to sell it, or restore it?'" Tom says, is one of the most difficult aspects about owning this car. "When I say 'Neither,' they shake their heads and walk away."

And the reason this Shelby is never going to be repainted or restored as long as Tom and Jim own it? "A car is only original once," Tom remarked. "Once a car is restored, it becomes more of a replica than an original car. Americans have a nasty habit of making old things look new, when in fact old things should look old . . . and proud. Like an elderly human, old cars should proudly wear their wrinkles."

The original Shelby GT500 badge on the lower front fender remains in decent condition as do the Shelby Owners Association and SCCA decals on the trunk lid. Unfortunately, the chrome on the rear bumper is beyond salvation.

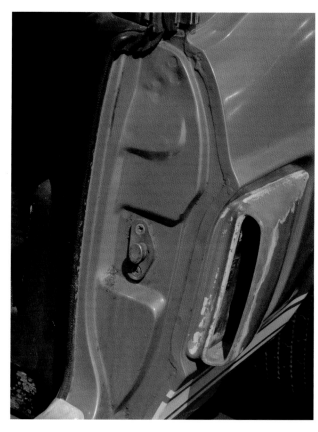

The factory-applied green paint has weathered throughout the body, the hood and its dual black stripes, the doorjambs, and the rear deck lid. The inside driver's-side doorjamb shows how the lower white stripe was originally installed.

From the instruments and steering wheel to the entire door panel assembly, everything on the inside of this Shelby has remained just as it was installed more than 40 years ago. The odometer reads 34,569 miles. Note the car's registration, which has remained wrapped around the steering column all these years.

Although most of the black finish has flaked off the aluminum air cleaner housing, it's a Shelby-original housing, as are both valve covers, oil filler tube cap, hoses, clamps, coil and, we believe, the distributor cap. The same goes for the original 10-spoke wheels.

Bona Fide Bowtie

If ever there exists the world's most perfectly original 1968 Chevrolet Chevelle SS 396, this is it.

IMAGINE THIS SCENARIO: You are 22 years old, you just bought a brand-new 1968 Chevelle SS 396, the muscle car wars are getting hotter by the minute, and Englishtown Raceway Park is just a short drive from your house. Yet, amazingly, you have absolutely no desire to take your big-block Chevelle down the drag strip. Not even once? Well, for original owner David Dodd of Boonton, New Jersey, the thought of racing his Chevy never entered his mind. Only nonstop care, fastidious cleaning, maintenance, and thoughtful safeguarding against the rigors of Mother Nature were always first and foremost on his young mind. He did everything he could to ensure that his beloved Chevelle would be kept in the best possible condition, and state of originality, that is humanly possible. If you can see this incredible time machine up close, you too would agree that David has achieved that goal.

David ordered the car on May 27, 1968, his 22nd birthday, taking delivery of it six weeks later on July 12. "My friend's dad, who helped me order the car, gave me a chamois and a sponge when the car was new," David fondly remembers. "He also gave me a book called *How to Care for Your Car* two years earlier. I remember read-

ing in the book about appearance and if kept clean and polished a car would look good for years. When the car was a few years old, I was still being asked if I just bought a new car."

Although it was David's original intention to use the Chevelle as his daily driver, after he got caught in the snow and discovered that big-block Chevelles have poor traction, he retired it from winter use. "In December 1968, I got caught in the snow and found that the car would only go sideways on the slightest of inclines," David said. "The following year, I was going somewhere when it started snowing, so I returned home and the car was put away until the snow season was over. It has been garaged ever since."

Thanks to the advice of his friends, and memories of driving in an SS 396 back when he was in the U.S. Naval Reserves, David ordered not only the L-78 SHPE (Special High Performance Engine) but also the M-22 close-ratio four-speed transmission. The exterior color is the rarely seen Grotto Blue, which is complemented nicely with black vinyl bucket seats, console, factory gauges, and the one-year-only barrel-type tach.

When the topic of original versus restored arose during our conversation, David was quite adamant in his thoughts on the subject: "The unrestored vehicle is an indispensable resource to restorers today. It shows the way these cars were actually built. They were production-line cars, built by workers just doing their jobs. They were not

The factory-applied Grotto Blue paint and white pinstripes look as if they were just applied. The black vinyl roof is original to the car as well—the fact that the top and bottom seams of the vinyl don't align is proof that this is a factory-installed top.

perfect in any way. Some examples on the Chevelle are the lack of paint on the steering wheel hub and on a piece of interior trim. The passenger door had to be adjusted because it was hitting the fender when opened and the pinstripes end at different heights at the rear of the car. I read in the owner's manual that cars with AM/FM radios received a fixed-length 31-inch antenna mast, but my Chevelle came with an adjustable mast. So I showed the manual to the dealer and the correct 31-inch mast was ordered."

Replacement parts that have been fitted to the car were done so only out of necessity. One valve spring and the speedometer cable were replaced in 1969, followed by the shocks—which were replaced with the correct Delco units—and a windshield in 1970. Because the reverse lock-out stopped working in 1972, the shifter—but not the original handle—was replaced. A new voltage regulator was put in back in 1973, and in 1989 both the fuel pump and driver's-side door glass had to be replaced. A new brake master cylinder was installed in 2005, followed a year later by two reproduction V belts. All of the original parts that were taken off the car have been saved, including one of the original tires.

"The Chevelle was first entered in a car show in 1981," David recalled. "Back then very few spectators recognized it as a 'survivor.' There is much more appreciation for the car in the last few years because it has not been touched. Some interested people will look at the car

Some of the rarely seen original factory details include the yellow-tip dipstick that shows it was fitted to a big-block 396-ci engine, pollution control equipment (including air pump), and all the various firewall markings.

121

The untouched cabin provides a rare look into the way these Chevelles were assembled. The wood steering wheel, shifter knob, floor mats, upholstery and seat backs, door panels, headliner, and carpeting are all 100 percent genuine Chevrolet parts circa 1968.

then return for a second look, and in some cases bring a friend along to show him something on the car. Many people find it hard to believe that the paint is original, but to me the paint is one of, if not the most important part of a survivor-type car.

"The interior is in good condition except for the driver's bucket seat," David stated with a very humble tone in his voice. "The seat is worn on the edge and cracked in several spots. The clutch, brake, and gas pedals all show signs of wear. Nonetheless there have been many photographs taken of its details. At the ACES Chevellabration in Tennessee in 2007, a member had a Grotto Blue, black vinyl top, bucket seat 1968 SS 396 and he told me that he copied my car, using over 100 photographs of the car that he had taken the previous year.

"I have been told to repaint the engine and several other areas; this is something I refuse to do. The paint on the engine and under the hood is the most difficult part of maintaining the car's originality. If I had polished under the hood it would be in better shape today. The engine was kept clean, but the paint burned off. Several years ago at a Corvette club show I was told by a judge to 'repaint the engine and detail the car, and come back next year and you'll do better.' But to me, a car can be restored over and over but it's only original once."

Untouched original cars are needed to show restorers the exact way the factory built them. Be it the attachment of the fender to the firewall, the hood springs, heater box, or how the quarter panel was welded to the rear trunk panel, all provide insight into the way GM constructed their cars. And note how the black-painted rocker was masked from the upper body color and how the body panels were fitted and spot-welded together.

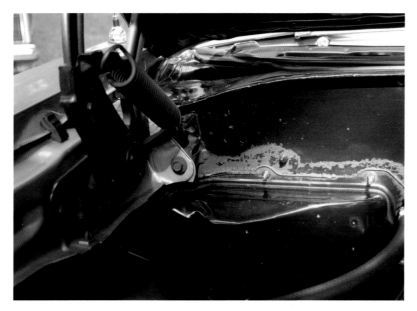

Sixties Flashback

*Three factory-original Mopars
that look the part.*

FAKE BLOOD, BLUDGEONED HEADS, crawling fingers, hairy-faced masks, and some of the scariest costumes ever created are the reason these three highly original Mopar muscle cars have been united. They are the primary focus of the collection belonging to one very serious Massachusetts Mopar fanatic, who, for the past 22 years, labored hard building his family-owned business into the huge success that it is today. The cars are a reward for all his hard work.

The Halloween Outlet in Worcester, Massachusetts, is one of the country's few superstores dedicated solely to Halloween costumes and supplies. Its owner is Gary Arvanigian, a muscle car enthusiast like few others I have ever met, and serious Halloween extremist. Gary came of age during the birth of the muscle car, an era in time that he has never forgotten. Now, thanks to the success of this store and the unwavering support of his family, he is able to relive those exciting days with cars that are the epitome of those tire-scorching times.

And just like the days of old, all of Gary's cars have to have that period-correct look. Five-spoke American Racing Torq-Thrusts wrapped with BFGoodrich tall sidewall blackwalls for that tough 1960s street-muscle appearance and bolted to slightly jacked-up suspensions are the perfect recipe for nostalgia. Throw in the fact that all of these Mopars are factory-built originals and it quickly becomes clear that Gary is a man with excellent taste.

"People's response when I tell them my cars are unrestored and my trying to convince them otherwise is both frustrating and fun," Gary said about owning original cars. "As time goes on, original cars are becoming a curiosity, so people are having a hard time taking it all in. But the best thing I like about these types of collector cars is that there are no stories; they are what they are. Even though quality restored cars are hard to beat, unrestored cars stand in a league of their own. Most important, they are a significant part of American history, and even though the temptation to 'overuse' them is apparent, sometimes it is hard to resist. I will, however, continue to preserve them in their original state, and savor their overall condition for as long as I own them."

1965 Dodge Coronet 500

Of all the 1965 Coronet 500 hardtops remaining on Earth, this Dodge is without question the absolute best of its kind. I spent a long time inspecting every square inch of this muscle machine and in the end I was simply blown away by its astonishing originality. From the white plastic clips holding the wiring harness to the firewall to the radiator hoses and spring clamps to the untouched bias-ply Goodyear spare tire that still wears its blue protective film over the white sidewall, everything is original to this car, making it a genuine original of the highest order. Even the orange "Paint OK" stamp on the passenger-side inner fender is in perfect condition.

Bought in 1997, Gary found out about the car through a friend of his. A West Coast car, it was sold in California by Stanley Dodge-Simca in National City. Spending most of its existence in the warm, rust-free climate before it headed east to Massachusetts, and driven less than 20,000 miles since new, means it has remained in exceptional shape. The Light Brown Poly exterior paint finish is as flawless as the day it was applied; it still wears a brilliant shine.

Inside, the two-tone tan and salmon vinyl upholstery is unbelievably perfect, with not a flaw in sight. The same goes for the carpet; yes, it too is the same carpet that this Coronet was built with. Underhood, the 426-ci "wedge" V8 still wears its original Carter four-barrel carburetor, manifolds, and just about every single mechanical and electrical component. Even the four-speed transmission is original to the car. As for those aftermarket wheels and tires, well, Gary has the originals stored in his warehouse.

"I have all the paperwork since day one," Gary said about this very unique Mopar. "This is a true benchmark car with Walter P. Chrysler museum potential."

It may be scratched, but the 426 decal applied to the engine's chrome rocker cover is a factory original. So too is everything else about this engine and its surrounding components, from the orange "PAINT OK" inspection stamp on the inner fender to the white plastic clips that hold the wiring harness in place.

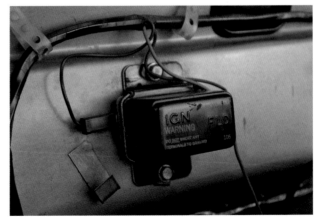

Due to the extensive amount of metal trim used in the interiors of these Coronets, chances are great that most show signs of corrosion or pitting. Not this Dodge. As you can see, this cabin looks as if it were just put together on the assembly line. Apart from a minor scratch or two, it's a look into Chrysler quality, circa 1965.

Although the American Racing wheels may not be correct, they enhance the Coronet with that tough 1960s-era street image. The original paint has that factory-produced orange peel finish that no restoration shop can duplicate, and inside the trunk resides the original Goodyear spare tire, which has never been used.

1966 Plymouth Satellite

As soon as he exited his Satellite once it was positioned for our photo shoot, Gary ran to the rear and popped open the trunk. "Wait until you see this," he said with great enthusiasm as he unlocked the trunk with the Plymouth's original key. "Take a close look at the spare tire; it's the original Bluestreak, and this is the original jack." Although I was surprised to see the original spare, even the gray plaid floor mat is original, and in very good condition, too. The factory-applied sound-deadening material sprayed onto the inner side of the rear quarter panels is still there, and all of it is in near perfect condition.

Like his Coronet 500, this is also a 20,000-mile car, although the 426-ci engine under the hood is a Hemi V8. Gary is the car's third owner, having bought it in 1992 just as his Halloween business started taking off. Upon close inspection, this Satellite is exactly the same as the day it rolled off the Plymouth assembly line. The two four-barrel Carter carburetors are there as is the Dana 60 rear end with highway friendly 3.50-ratio gears.

The black vinyl upholstered bucket seats are perfect, with not a single rip or scuff mark. So too is the chrome plating on the ribbed metal console. Even the chrome trim on the 6,000-rpm tach and surrounding the instrument cluster looks as if it were just plated. The dash top is crack-free perfect, the lettering on each gauge looks as if it were just silkscreened, and all four orange pointers remain bright in color. The tinted windshield is in equally fine condition, too. The only parts that have been replaced are the glass windshield washer bottle, the drive belts, and the radiator hoses.

Mopar fanatics will quickly notice that this gorgeous Plymouth still wears one of the rarest and hardest-to-find trim parts for Hemi-equipped Satellites built for this model year, and that's the metal trim panel on the trunk lid. With the inner portion painted red, this denotes it as a Hemi-spec piece, which is why it's so rare.

What's even more remarkable about this extraordinarily well-preserved Mopar is its exterior. Every square inch of that red paint is the very same enamel paint that the Chrysler workers sprayed on the car during its construction back in 1966, and it's literally perfect. So too is the paint just as flawless throughout both doorjambs and even on the vulnerable rocker panels, thus making this Hemi Satellite the absolute best of its kind.

Driven just 20,000 miles, it's no wonder the 426-ci Hemi engine still looks brand new. The original radiator hoses and clamps and the inspection marks never deteriorated, nor has any of the wiring or electrical connections.

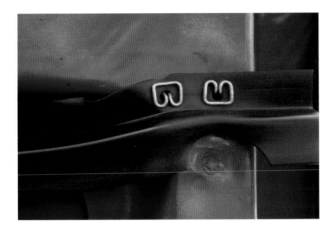

Due to regular maintenance, the weather stripping never got the chance to dry out. This hood strip remains held in place by the original clips. This long, thin mark left by the rear of the hood proves just how original this Satellite is, as does the oozing from below the sill plate of the factory-applied undercoating.

Padded dash top, simulated wood steering wheel, carpets, embossed seats, and door panels: all original to this car and all are in impeccable condition. The same applies to the console-mounted tach and shifter.

The sloppily applied seam sealer and sprayed-on sound deadening is just the way Plymouth assembled these cars. The original jack has hardly been used, and the blue-gray plaid floor mat is nearly stain free.

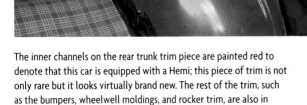

The inner channels on the rear trunk trim piece are painted red to denote that this car is equipped with a Hemi; this piece of trim is not only rare but it looks virtually brand new. The rest of the trim, such as the bumpers, wheelwell moldings, and rocker trim, are also in showroom-new shape.

1969 Road Runner

How's this for accolades? Certified "Unrestored Factory Stock" at the Mopar Nationals; two-time winner of the Carlisle All-Chrysler National's Survivor award; twice voted Best Mopar at the Mopar Nationals; and Voted "Fan Favorite" at Carlisle All-Chrysler Nationals, not to mention having been featured in *Mopar Action* magazine.

Yes, this triple black Road Runner is one of the best, and yes, it too is an original, unrestored Mopar. Sold by S. J. Reynolds Chrysler-Imperial-Plymouth dealer in Poughkeepsie, New York, Gary is the third owner. He bought it in 1997, with its odometer showing just 30,000 miles. Equipped with option A12, which is the 440-ci big-block V8 fitted with the highly desirable six-barrel multicarburetor setup of three Holley two-barrels, its drivetrain also includes a four-speed transmission and a stout Dana 60 Sure-Grip differential packing 4:10 gears.

Due to overly large slicks that were put on the car back in its day, the rear wheelwells were cut to make them fit. Being such a stickler for originality, Gary had the quarter panels repaired and the new paint carefully blended into the surrounding original paintwork. The work was done so well it's basically impossible to tell anything was done.

Other unique features to this incredible time capsule include the simulated wood grain sport steering wheel, tinted windows, three-speed windshield wipers, pop-out rear windows, cooling package, and the police handling package suspension. The Décor Group option includes custom style vinyl trim, B-pillar molding, rear arm rests and ashtrays, chrome armrest bases, chrome exhaust outlets, and chrome trim panel moldings. Throw in the radio delete plate and front bench seat, and the fact that all of these parts are in excellent original condition, and this Plymouth really is in a class all its own.

"I felt that an unrestored black on black on black six-pack Road Runner would be one of the most rare of its category," Gary told me while I was inspecting the fearsome Plymouth closely. "Although the car is nearly all original, I did change the wheels and tires from the factory redlines to that cool 1960s look of large sidewall blackwall tires with dog-dish hubcaps. However, when I removed the original wheels with the factory-installed redlines, I safely put them away in dry storage."

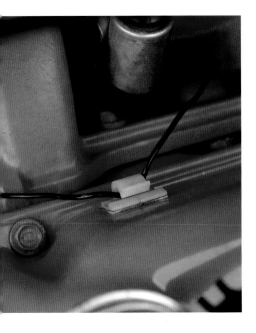

The 440-ci big-block is fitted with lots of rare original components that you won't readily find on other Road Runners; they include the Electronic Suppression spark plug wires, ignition coil, plastic clips, date-coded heater, and radiator hoses with their correct clamps and battery cables.

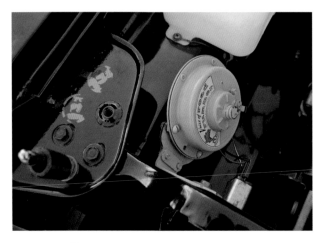

With the lift-off hood removed, it's easy to see the sloppily applied brown paint and bare copper clip. Factory inspection marks were stamped onto the hood pin support plate.

The Mopar Nationals don't grant you a Certified "Unrestored Factory Stock" award if your car doesn't meet their stringent guidelines. It is unmolested original interiors such as this that allowed this Road Runner to qualify.

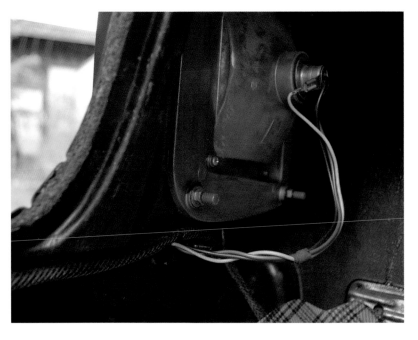

Other significant details include the trunk's original floor mat, hardly used G70-15 spare tire, and as-applied factory sound deadener on the inside quarter panels. Rarer still are the small red plastic plugs that cover the rear taillamp assembly studs.

One-Owner Original

A Pure Stock participant back in 1969, this authentic Chevrolet Camaro SS has traveled less than 22,000 miles since.

When I spotted this white Camaro sitting in the parking lot of *Hemmings Motor News* during one of our 2007 summer cruise nights, I could not believe the car's incredible originality. At first I thought that it had been repainted by an inexperienced amateur body-man because there were signs of poor body work—especially on the C-pillar—paint runs in the door jambs, and overspray throughout the firewall area. Then a closer inspection revealed that what I was looking at was General Motors quality, circa 1969. Even the black tailpanel shows how quickly the assembly-line workers fitted the mask to the body to spray on the flat black paint; the tell-tale signs are in the corners where the mask wasn't perfectly placed, thus allowing black overspray onto the surrounding white finish. It's the little details such as these that make original cars so historically important.

James House Jr. of Averill Park, New York, ordered this Camaro on May 16, 1969, when he was just 24 years old. The deal he and his wife made was a simple one: He could buy a new Camaro, but only if it was equipped with an automatic transmission so she could drive it. "When I saw what the new second-generation Camaro was going to look like I didn't care for it, and I knew this would be my last chance to get a new Camaro

with the early body style that I preferred."

When he walked into the Chevrolet showroom, James knew exactly what he wanted. He ordered the SS option with a white body and blue interior and the optional fold-down rear seat. Equipped with the L78 396-ci V8 that was factory rated at 375 horsepower, it's amazing that young James didn't abuse the car like most others did, although he did race it in the Pure Stock class at nearby Lebanon Valley dragway. Instead, he took care of it and babied it; perhaps this is why the odometer shows a mere 21,700 miles clocked so far. More important, the interior is in excellent condition, with not a single trace of anything being worn.

The list of mechanical parts that have been replaced through the years is relatively short: rear shocks, 1969; tires, 1970; carburetor and lower radiator hose, 1983; battery, 2006; chambered exhaust system, valve covers, air filter cover, radiator cap, floor mats, spark plug wires, and fuel pump, August 2007. Thankfully, James kept all the original parts that he took off his Camaro, including the original exhaust system, and stored them in a safe place.

"Keeping it in good running order and rodent-free," is the part of maintaining the car's originality that James finds most difficult. Yet, not being a man of many words, James got right to the point when I asked him his thoughts on owning this original collector car: "I have tried to keep it in good shape and apparently it has worked."

Factory markings are evident everywhere. These green Bs are on the firewall above the brake master cylinder, while the original upper radiator hose still shows its factory numbers; the clamp is also original to this car.

When built, the Camaro's construction details were less than stellar. Glue has remained on the driver's-side doorjamb, the tail panel shows how sloppy it was taped off prior to being painted black, and the side stripe's outline stripe was cut off below the "396" badge.

The material that GM used inside their cars has always been a premium product. Here we see just how well the door panels, front seat upholstery, and optional rear fold-down seat have held up. The console and its optional gauges have remained in perfect condition.

With 375 horsepower on tap, the 350-ci V8 has never been removed from the car. In fact, aside from the nonoriginal valve covers, nothing on the engine has ever been taken apart. The aluminum foil surrounding the heater hoses was put there in 1970, and has stayed ever since.

Genuine GS

A rolling time capsule of Flint's finest workmanship can be discovered in this untouched 1970 Buick Skylark GS.

WHEN THE TELEVISION SHOW *Pinks* held one of its legendary heads-up competitions at upstate New York's Lebanon Valley Raceway back in October 2007, a local Buick enthusiast came out on top. With his family and friends cheering him on, Nelson Belot from Pittsfield, Massachusetts, won it all in his 455-powered 1971 Buick Skylark.

Being an automotive machinist and engine builder has its advantages, especially when you need to keep a small collection of muscle cars in peak performance. Inside his expansive metal-sided garage in the Berkshire countryside, next to his original Chevy Vega, 1966 big-block El Camino, Chevelles, Camaros, and a 1965 GTO, resides his most cherished Detroit street machine, this 1970 Buick GS hardtop.

GS Buicks of this vintage are getting quite hard to come by these days, especially one like this that's literally a 99 percent factory original. From its Aqua Mist paint and black interior, to its 350-ci V8 and Turbo 350 automatic transmission, it's nothing short of a rolling museum of Flint's finest craftsmanship. Even the Rochester four-barrel carburetor is original to the car.

"Some of the seat stitching is coming apart, but the rest of the interior is near flawless," Nelson said of his good-looking GS. "The water pump and battery have been replaced and the exhaust system was replaced with a factory-exact replica from Gardiner. Thankfully, some of the hardest-to-find parts for these GS Buicks, such as the factory air cleaner and wheels, are not only still with the car but all are in excellent condition, too."

Driven just 47,000 miles, Nelson found this GS listed for sale on eBay, and just couldn't resist the temptation of adding it to his collection. "It's an unrestored, original-paint muscle car that runs and drives like new. The whole car is a time capsule," he says. "Just keeping it running, clean, and preventing people from scratching it by accident when they want to take a close look at it are the toughest things about maintaining the car in its original state. That is why, to help preserve the paint and the interior as best I can, whenever I take the car out I make sure to never park it in the sun.

"It's funny, only serious car nuts like us like unrestored cars. Most people like the lipstick look, where everything has to be shiny and perfect, but in my eyes, cars like my Buick are only original once."

The well-preserved speckle painat finish on the trunk hinges details exactly how the BUick workers sprayed it on.

Be it the foam that seals the ram air tracts, the brake master cylinder, or the red paint on both valve covers, everything you see here is authentic Buick. The undercoating surrounding the heater box may look sloppily applied, but that too was done by the factory.

The GS's rather plain Jane interior is in unbelievable condition for being 100 percent original. There's not a split on the dash top, a rip in the upholstery, or a tear in the carpet. In addition to the original floor mats, what's most remarkable is that the paper Engine Starting Procedure instructions installed by a Buick worker onto the driver's-side sun visor has never been removed.

Feast your eyes on this, GS fans. Both front grilles are factory originals; so, too, are the two smaller grilles in the hood. And not a single grille is cracked, which is a rarity today.

Middle Village Mopars

Deep in the heart of this congested New York City neighborhood lie two of the best unrestored Mopars known to exist.

IN A NEIGHBORHOOD where the houses are not only all attached but where each residence is barely 12 feet wide, to find even one serious collector-car enthusiast within its borders would be considered quite surprising. More amazing would be a muscle car collector who owns not one, not two, but five of the most desirable Detroit street machines ever built. And they're all smack dab in the heart of Middle Village, Queens, a short 15-minute drive from midtown Manhattan.

Meet John Scalfani, Mopar fanatic extraordinaire. If ever one can be considered a Mopar maniac, John's your man. Besides this 1970 Dodge Super Bee and 1971 'Cuda, both of which are unrestored originals, he also owns a 1970 Challenger R/T Hemi and a 1971 R/T Challenger 383; a 1970 Boss 429 Mustang is his only non-Mopar toy. And his den is filled with all sorts of Moparmobilia including an original Super Bee wall fixture that's almost the length of his couch below.

While other enthusiasts may own more Mopars, to possess such rare, hard-to-store items when your house has only a single-car garage—and the price to rent garage space is astronomically high—takes an amazing amount of fortitude to stay the course. Sure, John can make life easy for himself and his wife by selling the cars

or by, perish the thought, moving to the suburbs to allow him more space, but this NYC-bred boy just won't leave the city, nor will he give up his Mopars. Especially the two well-preserved originals featured here.

"Not everyone can own an unrestored car," says Scalfani. "Most hobbyists or collectors want shiny over-restored vehicles to display at major car events, but I prefer cars that are original.

"There are no issues with unrestored cars. They ride better, and the orange peel in the paint is correct as to how they were painted right out of the factory with poor quality control. Unrestored cars have character, and represent a time that cannot be duplicated today."

1970 Dodge Super Bee

"This is a perfect example of a muscle car time capsule, and one of the best examples of a 1970 Super Bee Plum Crazy original-paint car." That is John's assessment of his beloved Super Bee, a statement that I have to completely agree with. "Besides the paint, the exhaust system is original, too, and the engine and transmission have never been out of the car—that's what I like most about it."

When John found the car, in his words it was "a solid #2 condition car." The Dodge came with all the essential credentials that Mopar collectors must have when purchasing such rare finds. It was a complete, numbers-matching car with full documentation that included the

original window sticker and build sheet; the odometer read just 20,700 miles. As an added bonus it still had its original air filter and all eight original sparks plugs.

Better still, all the other hard-to-find Dodge-installed parts are still on this car, including all the hoses, negative and positive battery cables, and correct date-coded shocks front and rear. And it's those very same hoses, along with the belts and the exhaust system, that John finds are the most difficult parts to maintain for the car to stay as original as possible, although back in 1984 the gas tank was replaced by the original owner, followed only recently by new tires and brakes.

"Once I realized just how significant this car really was, my two main goals were to preserve a piece of history and display it at All-Chrysler Nationals in the Mopar Survivor tent. I keep the exterior waxed, silicone the vinyl top, and use a cleaner to protect the vinyl interior. A car cover protects the body and I use DampRids, those moisture absorbers that you hang, to absorb any moisture present. And to avoid wear on the gas and brake pedals I keep the pedals covered with socks."

It may look like a professionally restored interior but it's anything but. This is what nearly 40-year-old upholstery, console, carpet, gauges, and trim look like when they've only been used 20,700 miles, and are meticulously cared for.

Every speck of purple, orange, and black paint you see here was applied by Dodge back in 1970. The 335-horsepower 383-ci Magnum V8, its four-barrel Holley carb, and 727 TorqueFlite automatic have all remained untouched. All the original electrical components and wiring are in excellent shape, and all eight original spark plugs, showing the orange engine-paint overspray on them, have been saved for posterity.

The original Goodyear Polyglas F70-14 spare tire has never touched the ground, nor has the accompanying jack ever been used.

Just a run-of-the-mill production car when it was built, when the weather stripping along the trunk's rain channel was originally installed, some assembly-line worker applied just a tad too much adhesive. Even more special to see is the light blue dab of paint atop the front shock stud; only original, factory-installed shocks had this paint on them.

1971 Plymouth 'Cuda

If you own a garage in Queens, chances are the entrance to your space is part of a community driveway. This is a single-lane driveway that's located behind the house and runs the length of the entire block connecting to all the backyards and garages. Seeing where this 'Cuda resides, it was only appropriate that we photographed the car there. As you can see, it's quite the challenge to be a car enthusiast when you're living in such an anti–car friendly environment.

I've been invited to view several unrestored 'Cudas, and without question this is one of the best-kept all-original examples I've ever had the chance to inspect. As John puts it: "It's one of the finest examples of a '71 'Cuda in the hobby. It's an absolute survivor with full documentation, the original bill of sale and broadcast sheet, matching-numbers engine and transmission, original paint and billboards and interior."

This Tor Red 'Cuda lived most of its life out in the dry climate of California. Then John spotted it listed for sale on heminet.com and in February 2004 became its next owner. "Like the Super Bee, it too is a solid #2 condition car. The engine and exhaust system needs to be refreshed, but other than that overall it's a solid, numbers-matching vehicle."

Being a 24,500-mile car means that little, if anything, needs to be done to it; however, the Carter four-barrel Thermo-Quad carb could benefit from a rebuild. And finding original-spec E60-15-size polyglas tires is proving quite the challenge.

"Cars like this represent a part of muscle car history, and portray to the restorer and collector how they were made without much quality control," John thoughtfully replied when I asked him his opinion about unrestored cars verses restored ones. "An unrestored car has no issues, all numbers match, all doors and locks close. The exterior paint with its inherent orange-peel finish provides a certain character that only original cars have. More important, not everyone can be a caretaker of unrestored cars."

The steering wheel, upholstery, floor mats, seat belts, and dash pad—all well-kept original components that make this 'Cuda one of the most authentic of its breed. The one-piece door panels too are free of any marks or scratches.

The mark of a well-maintained car is an engine compartment that is so clean you can practically eat off its surrounding sheet metal—this is such an example. The 275-horsepower 340-ci V8 has never been apart, and the 727 TorqueFlite shifts with the same authority it had when the car was first built.

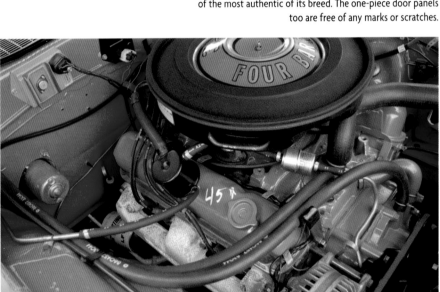

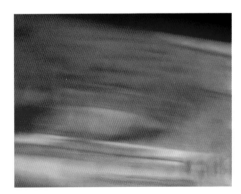

These are the construction details that restorers are keen to see so they can duplicate them on their own restoration projects, thus restoring their cars to the most accurate standards. But even then they would just be replicas of the real thing.

Factory-installed original-equipment parts such as these are what make cars like this so desirable to own. The valence-mounted turn-signal lenses, exhaust tips with the original tailpipe protruding through, and the space-saver spare with its companion bottle inflator are all highly sought-after parts.

Highway Star

From day one, this 1971 Ford Mustang has been specifically maintained to last a lifetime.

506,040.7 MILES. As of December 2007, that's how many miles this unrestored Mustang had been driven. Its owner, Dick Fuchs, a highly creative inventor of mechanical items such as electric drills, hand tools, and engine testing equipment, is the original owner. So too is the paint original, as is the engine, transmission, differential, gauges, and interior upholstery and carpeting.

A very meticulous owner, the kind that keeps strict maintenance records, Dick has two large binders filled with intensive data that he has recorded since day one of ownership. Whenever he returned home from driving the car, he wrote down such detailed information as mileage driven, amount of time that the engine was in operation, amount of gas consumed, including its octane rating and price, average speed and time of the trip, and outside temperature. The end result of all this fanatical record keeping and the ensuing protection and preservation of the car's originality has rendered it perhaps the best-kept, high-mileage Mustang in existence.

Dick, who hails from Simsbury, Connecticut, specially ordered this black and Argent silver-striped hardtop model with the 351 Ram Air V8 and Hurst-shifted Top-Loader four-speed transmission. He took delivery of it on February 13, 1971, from McCormack Ford in Beacon, New York. The odometer registered 13 miles.

Being the clever character that he is, Dick said, "When I bought the car it was new, but 'partially assembled' by the Ford Motor Company. There were so many deficiencies, 'rebuilding' started almost immediately. As an example, one week after delivery I had to put the correct pitman shaft seal in the steering box to stop the lube from leaking onto the ground."

The reasons why Dick ordered the car the way he did were many. "It was the 'last' of the 'muscle cars.' I wanted the largest-cubic-inch-displacement engine that wasn't really 'high performance' with a four-speed transmission and the lowest rear-axle ratio for long life and good fuel mileage with decent over-the-road performance. I made this car that way by changing from a 3.25 to 2.75:1 rear gear ratio at 16,793 miles. It's the best over-the-road car that I have ever driven or ridden in, and I appreciate its economical longevity."

Besides the Mustang's unique specifications and ride quality, Dick loves the way it sounds. "I like my custom-built exhaust sound. The original system, which I still have, seemed louder, however." That custom exhaust was made of mild steel and installed 25 years ago; to date it has been on the car for more than 300,000 miles. The reason it remains rust free, as does the Mustang's entire body and floor pan, is because the car is not driven from November through April, and seldom in the rain. Dick is also quite proud of the fact that when the odometer showed almost 506,000 miles, the AACA

Residing under the car's original Ram Air hood, which still sports the factory-applied black and silver paint, is a 351-ci Cleveland V8 that's lived well beyond the lifespan that even Ford engineers expected it to. A backup oil filter and water separator were installed when the car was new, thus positively impacting the engine's longevity.

The front crossmember, as well as the entire floor pan, is completely free of any corrosion, and all because it was rarely driven in the rain and never when snow was on the road. That is why the original black paint and all the factory inspection markings have survived so well—the same reason the trunk floor, inner wheel wells, and lower quarter panels are all rust free.

awarded his Mustang their Historic Preservation of Original Features designation at the 2007 Northeast Regional Meet held in Binghamton, New York.

If you use a car sparingly, maintaining its originality is a fairly easy task. But if you use the car daily and drive it an above-average amount of miles each year, then the job of preserving the car's originality becomes an almost insurmountable undertaking. "Making —and repairing—the car the way it should have been assembled has been most difficult," Dick said. "Now, the hard part is finding certain reasonably priced replacement parts. The large-port Cleveland cylinder heads had a valve job because of the unleaded fuels and a new camshaft drive at 200,000 miles. The brake shoes were replaced at 200,000 miles, too, yet the drums not only still look new but they are original to the car.

"At 300,000 miles the engine had a major overhaul: this included hardened exhaust valve seats, a rebore with new pistons, a new camshaft, and another new cam drive due to a cracked piston caused by the poor-quality fuels. The radiator and heater cores have been replaced, but the coolant, radiator, and heater hoses are

original, as are the PCV valve, carburetor, and distributor. I also had to repair the right rear axle. When Ford made it, they ground the outboard wheel bearing area askew so the bearings would not last. I had it ground down, metal sprayed, reground, and a new bearing installed, and have not had any problems since."

As to the desirability of unrestored originals, with conviction, Dick stated: "There can be only one first time. Repairs, yes, but completely disassembling a vehicle and restoring it to its original condition is never possible. After a car has been restored it can never be placed back to original condition."

Unlike most people who bought a car to fill a need for transportation, Dick said that his original intention when he bought the Mustang was "to keep it 'original' for at least 400,000 miles and for low-cost operation. But, 400,000 miles seemed to arrive rather quickly, so I keep driving it. I plan to keep it and maintain it as I have for as long as I can. This is the only car I have ever owned that has risen in value by a factor of three over the purchase price, even with the high mileage!"

Stepping into the interior, you'll find the original stainless Ford sill plates covering rocker panels that have zero rust on them. The factory door panels may not have any rips, but the telltale dark areas resulted from more than a half-million miles of arm and hand motions, although the Mustang Recommended Tire Pressure sticker still looks new.

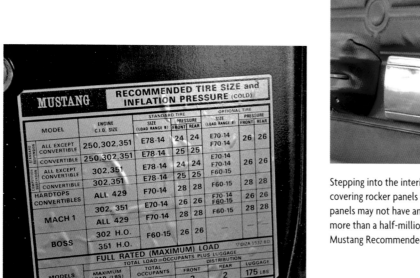

141

Magnum Opus

*Few Dodge Chargers remain in such
original shape, yet this 1971 R/T has been
driven 130,000 miles and survived.*

THE NORTHEAST REGION of the United States is a venerable hotbed of interesting Mopars. Walk the showfield during the 4,000-car-strong All-Chrysler Nationals in Carlisle, Pennsylvania, in July and you'll see a huge number of the more appealing Mopars with license plates from all throughout New England and adjoining upstate New York. There, in the Capital Region of Albany, and its surrounding farming communities and resort towns, you'll find more than your average number of significant, unrestored vintage Mopars stashed in weathered barns and warm garages.

On the outskirts of the town of Saratoga resides this incredibly well-preserved 1971 Dodge Charger R/T. Its white paint, black upholstery, and powerful big-block V8 remain today just as they were sprayed, stitched, and assembled nearly 40 years ago. To the many fuselage Charger fans in the region who have seen this car, it represents an important window into how these highly collectible B-body muscle cars were really built.

"My primary objective when I bought this car was to drive it for five years and then restore her," its owner, longstanding Mopar fanatic Pete Silic, said. "But so many people have told me I would ruin the car if she was restored. The more I think about it, the more I realize they are right. The main reason I fell in love with her, besides the white color, was because she was untouched.

"There was no rust on the car at all. There are, however, more than a hundred little dents, scratches, and chipped-paint spots. "The interior is in excellent condition, the six-way powered houndstooth cloth-upholstered driver's seat has some wear on it, and the carpet definitely shows its age, but it all looks very satisfactory. Still, the old Dodge is amazingly presentable from 10 feet away. Up close, looking at all her little imperfections is perhaps the hardest part of owning such an original car."

Back in the 1980s, Pete owned several worthwhile Mopars, well before they were considered worthy collector cars. "I had a 1973 Dodge Charger and a 1971 Plymouth GTX when I was a kid, but I unfortunately sold them," Pete remembers. "Perhaps this is why I wanted another Charger. You always try to get what you had when you were younger. Maybe that's why when I'm driving this Charger it makes me feel like I'm young again. More important, there's nothing like going down the road in an old car."

This particular Charger R/T sports the highly desirable 370-horsepower 440-ci Magnum V8 and the robust 727 TorqueFlite automatic transmission. Besides the powertrain working as smoothly as the day it was first

assembled, so too do the power windows work as perfectly as the day their motors were first installed. Only the rear valance has been replaced, sometime during the car's existence in Texas where it spent all of its previous life accumulating its more than 128,000 miles.

Today, Pete drives his rolling automotive artifact about 2,000 miles annually, which amounts to about once or twice a week during the summer, or when he's driving to either the Adirondack Nationals or Musclepalooza at Lebanon Valley Raceway. "When I'm showing the Charger at a car show and there's the same car as mine that's been restored, my Dodge is the one that usually gets the most attention."

And speaking of restored cars verses original cars, Pete was quite realistic about his thoughts on the subject. "When you look at a car that has been restored you don't know a lot of time what's underneath all that fresh paint. The car might be hiding a lot of secrets."

From the Carter four-barrel carburetor and Transistorized ignition module to the plastic windshield washer water container and the black "R/T" hood striping, every component is a factory original, including the Rallye wheels, trim rings, and center caps.

Slightly worn but oh so original, everything in the interior is factory correct. So, too, are the Rim-blow steering wheel and the very rare Mopar cassette player and recording microphone, which still work perfectly. Even the rear seats, door panels, and woodgrain insert have withstood the test of time quite well.

From the 440 Magnum emblems to the black R/T hood decal to the plastic overflow container and rear exhaust tips, everything has remained as installed circa 1971. The rear taillamp covers may have weathered slightly, but they show exactly how Chrysler had them refinished.

Golden Chariots

With three other Pontiac GTOs in his collection, being the original owner of this 1972 GTO makes its ownership all the more special—and there's an unrestored 1955 Bel Air, too.

WHEN HE WAS A high school student back in the mid-1960s, Ralph Russo of Bohemia, New York, drove around in a red 1965 GTO hardtop. The car's calling card was a distinctive two-GTO-emblem front end—one emblem on the right grille, the other on the left grille. Nearly 45 years later, he still owns that same car.

A few years into his first job he had saved enough money to buy a new car, so, with his uncle's connections, he drove to Star Pontiac on Staten Island in October 1971 where he bought this 1972 GTO, his first new car.

Equipped with the standard 400, four-barrel V8, this GTO has remained exactly the way it rolled off the assembly line. Nothing has been touched nor has anything been changed. It's only been driven 29,000 miles, which is why it still drives as solidly as any new car built today.

With a second 1965 GTO hardtop built up with period mods, followed by a 1966 GTO convertible, in 1987 Ralph had the opportunity to add this very original 1955 Chevrolet Bel Air four-door sedan to his collection. Seeing just how original the Chevy was he didn't need to think twice about it; he bought it on the spot due to his deep appreciation for unrestored collector cars.

Whenever the sun's shining and the roads are dry, Ralph will fire up its small-block V8 and drive over to his shop, Avenue Automotive in Bohemia, where he spends his days repairing and restoring collector cars for a select group of discerning car owners. Like his 1972 GTO, he says that the Bel Air rides extremely well for its age, and never gives him an ounce of trouble.

"I keep all my cars garaged so they are never exposed to the harsh elements, which is a difficult task in and of itself, especially when you live on Long Island where safe storage is at a premium," Ralph said. "A garage is vital if the car has not been restored and you want to maintain its authenticity. An open checkbook is all that's needed to restore a car, but it takes real dedication to keep an original car in original condition."

1972 Pontiac GTO

With the red ribbon still wrapped around the steering column since the day it was first brought home, the condition of this GTO's interior simply boggles the mind. From the perfectly preserved woodgrain appliqué to the condition of the steering wheel, upholstery, carpets, and dashpad, you would be amazed as just how well everything has survived. And the optional 8-track tape player still works!

This is how an untouched, completely authentic 1972 GTO engine compartment is supposed to look. Nothing has been touched or altered; the factory-applied inspection mark remains on the firewall and, if you look closely, the brake booster still has the "WK" paper tag on it. And, yes, that's the original date-coded radiator hose and clamp.

The dealer's metal license plate frame has never been removed nor has the exhaust system, including both mufflers, ever been replaced. The original spare tire was used just once, thus most of the yellow and green markings on the treads are still visible.

1955 Bel Air

The original carpets may be worn and discolored and the steering wheel's finish partially worn away, yet the interior still retains that original factory appearance that so many owners wish their restored cars had. The seats, too, are still covered in the factory fabric and neither has a tear in them.

The 265-ci engine, Chevy's first small-block V8, still purrs along nicely and has never needed any repairs. Aside from a new fuel pump and some hoses, clamps, and filters all has remained just as Chevrolet assembled it.

The stainless trim pieces have no dents, nor are the painted sections worn away, although the gold Bowtie emblem has tarnished a bit. There are several areas on the body where the original paint has worn down to the primer coat, proving just how honest this Chevy's body really is. And the bluedot taillamp lenses are replacements for the original lenses that have been stored for safekeeping.

Collectible Colonnade

A 1973 Chevrolet Chevelle SS that survived the 1970s, and well beyond.

Big PROTRUDING BUMPERS and emissions-saddled powertrains. If ever there was an era when cars were looked upon as nothing more than disposable transportation objects, the model years of 1973 and beyond were it. Cars were not cared for with the same loving attention as those automotive offerings that came before them, so it is quite a rare occurrence today to discover a Colonnade-styled car with not only less than 50,000 miles on its odometer but one that is 99 percent original.

Found listed for sale in the September 2001 issue of *Hemmings Motor News* by its current owner, Joe Fina, a transplanted New Yorker now living in Florida, this tastefully designed Chevrolet was originally purchased in Kansas City, Missouri, then spent most of its existence in North Carolina. The first owner ordered this Chevelle SS with the Z15 option, which included the blacked-out grille, color-keyed lower body striping, G70x14 radial tires with raised white lettering fitted onto Rally wheels, and dual sport mirrors. And being the performance-car type that he was, he also checked off the LS4 option, which equipped the car with the 454-ci big-block V8; approximately 2,100 SSs for the 1973 model year were ordered with this engine. Rarer still, the fact that it was also ordered with the optional M21 close-ratio manual four-speed transmission means that

this is one of about 600 Chevelles produced with this highly entertaining power combination.

Aside from the car's most noteworthy feature, the swing-out Strato front bucket seats, it is also equipped with Posi-Traction, air conditioning, seat belt/shoulder belt combination, console, tilt steering wheel, AM/FM stereo, bumper guards, tinted glass and rear defroster, power steering, auxiliary lighting, special instrumentation, heavy-duty battery, and the F40 Special Suspension package, which includes front and rear anti-roll bars.

Of course the single most significant feature of this handsomely styled Chevelle SS is its originality. This car today is exactly the way it rolled off the Chevrolet assembly line. Apart from the usual wearing items like battery, fan belts, and tires, everything else about this automobile is just as the Chevrolet workers built it.

"Luckily, the car came to me in excellent condition," Joe stated. "It was pretty much delivered as you see it. I just had to do a lot of detailing on the car. It is a good thing, because all of the parts are hard to come by. The aftermarket seems to have ignored them completely.

"After selling two high-dollar cars to pay for the kid's college and a wedding, I wanted something less expensive, and quite frankly, I got tired of seeing the same old thing. I wanted something different. I always liked this body style, and looked around for either a Laguna Type S-3 or an SS. Because most enthusiasts are focused on the 1968–1972 body style, I figured I could buy a rare

car like this at a reasonable price. The biggest problem was finding one."

The biggest dilemma one has with owning such an original automotive artifact such as this is the simple fact that it is irreplaceable. "At this point, I only drive the car about 200 miles per year. It is kept in a garage under a cover," Joe sadly reported. "Unfortunately, with a car this original, I am scared to take it out on the road too often. It is only original once."

The blue vinyl upholstery is just about perfect, with nary a split or stain; the same for the carpeting and the Fisher-badged sill trim. Ditto for the black steering wheel, gauges, radio, shifter, and shifter knob. Literally everything on this car is factory original, and all of it—thanks to its two caring owners—remains in excellent condition.

The net-rated 245-horsepower V8 sports the same components that it was first assembled with including the original Quadrajet, all the power-robbing emissions equipment, and all the OE date-coded vacuum hoses, wiring, clamps, and fasteners that the car was first assembled with. Because the engine has never needed any repairs, none of the bolts and nuts had ever had a wrench or socket touch them since they were first screwed into place.

The blue paint is the very same paint applied by Chevrolet, and it is still in excellent condition; the paint splotch on the front fender below the 454 badge was done at the factory. Even the silver, color-keyed lower body side striping is still in excellent condition, as are the chrome and rubber inserts on the bumpers and all the surrounding chrome window trim and tinted glass.

Chapter 6

The Gold Standard: Bloomington Gold's Survivors

Perhaps the ultimate reward for owners of original Corvettes is obtaining Survivor Certification from Bloomington Gold. This is the standard by which all other Corvettes, as well as many other collector-car shows, are judged.

Bloomington Gold has been the hobby's leading force of authenticating unrestored original Corvettes since the late 1980s, and are now branching out to extend their Survivor Certification process to include all collector cars, both American and foreign.

Being certified by Bloomington Gold doesn't mean that your original car is the best of its kind, but having its condition professionally validated will provide your car with an added-value advantage over those cars that have not been certified. Either way, it's great to see the recognition of automotive originality being taken so seriously.

Corvette owners and collectors lead the pack when it comes to appreciating preservation thanks to the success of Bloomington Gold, the world's pre-eminent showcase for these original gems.

Photographs courtesy of David Burroughs

Golden Chariots

Bloomington Gold, the Corvette event where the term "Survivor" was coined.

BLOOMINGTON GOLD trademarked the word "Survivor" back in 1990 to protect their judging process for unrestored original Corvettes. According to the Bloomington Gold Web site: "If anyone looks through *Hemmings* (*Motor News*) or similar car magazines before we trademarked its usage, Survivor will not be found. It has only been since our introduction in 1990 that many others have begun using it generically to describe unrestored automobiles.

"People can use other words to describe their cars: Unrestored, Genuine, Original, etc. But Survivor is our trade name and cannot be used unless it has been through our process. Our Survivor brand stands for something that adds value to cars…competent judges have evaluated them and determined them to be over 50% unrestored original and in good condition. Our process certifies this and we put our third party stamp on it.

"Owners of true Survivor cars that have gone through our process can advertise their cars this way and the people who read those ads can be confident they are not reading someone's self-described hype. This is how it benefits the marketplace."

So, what exactly is a Survivor? Any model Corvette can apply for Survivor status, but it must be at least 20 years old. Prior to judging, it must complete a 25.4-mile road test to ensure that it performs as Chevrolet built it, and without any problems. The car itself must remain over 50 percent unrestored or unmodified in at least three out of the four following areas: interior, exterior paint and body, chassis, and engine/underhood. And the final requirement is that the judges must feel the car is an excellent educational example for future restoration projects.

I attended Bloomington Gold in the mid-1990s when it was held at the fairgrounds in Springfield, Illinois, and was amazed at the scope of the event. From the selection of show cars and parts for sale to the actual judging teams, you can't find a more serious, professionally run event. Most of the Survivor Corvettes were truly spectacular, and were excellent examples of the breed that would allow future restorations of similar-model Corvettes to be accomplished in the most authentic, factory-correct manner. Thus, the collector-car hobby owes a great debt to the Bloomington Gold folks for elevating the importance and respectability of old cars that have not been restored or modified.

During the judging of this unrestored, fuel-injected, solid-axle Corvette in the 1953–1962 class, the specially appointed Survivor judges regularly consulted with each other over certain details to ensure that the car is correctly evaluated.

The Bloomington Gold judging process is done in a most professional manner. Be it an early solid-axle model or a mid-year-era Sting Ray, the guiding principles used to evaluate every Corvette is the same.

From top to bottom and inside and out, every square inch of every Corvette is inspected by experts specializing in that particular model. Minitelescopes, like the one this Survivor judge is looking through, are used to view certain details up close.

Due to the extraordinary originality and sheer perfection of this Corvette, this is one instance where photographs truly are worth far more than words. So to avoid being repetitious (what other words can we possibly use besides "perfectly original" over and over again to describe its many details) study the photographs closely and you will see firsthand what a flawlessly preserved, all-original, solid-axle Corvette looks like. *Courtesy of Mike Yager.*

Solid-axle Survivor

The pride of Mike Yager's garage is this pristine 1954 Corvette.

ONE OF THE ABSOLUTE BEST original Corvettes in existence is this 1954 Pennant Blue model.

With a mere 3,073 miles on its odometer, it's the lowest-mileage all-original Corvette in existence: a true Bloomington Gold Survivor of the highest order.

Ultrarare cars such as this belong to those enthusiasts who appreciate them the most, thus it is only fitting that this solid-axle beauty belongs to the Corvette's biggest fan, Mike Yager.

As the founder of Mid America Motorworks, the most respected company specializing in parts and accessories for Corvettes and air-cooled Volkswagens, Mike also plays host to the world's largest event honoring Chevrolet's sports car, the Corvette Funfest. With some 12,000 Corvettes in attendance, it's a spectacle that all Corvette fans should attend at least once in their lives. I did in 1996, and I hope to visit there again in the very near future.

One of the main attractions at Funfest is My Garage, the building where Mike's collection of Corvettes and Corvettabilia is housed. His collection is quite selective, as every Corvette is a truly special machine, some of which are the only known examples. There's the 1964 coupe that was custom built for then Chevrolet General Manager Bunkie Knudsen; the 1964 New York World's Fair car that was a one-off styling exercise by Bill Mitchell and his design team; and the 1968 Le Mans Corvette that finished 15th overall at the 1972 24 Hours of Le Mans and finished First-in-Class at the 1972 and 1973 Daytona 24 Hours. There's also a 1989 pre-production LT-5 pilot car, 1 of only 6 existing ZR-1 prototypes. Then, of course, there's this incredible 1954 roadster.

Still registered in the name of its first owner, this Corvette is a 100 percent factory original. From its beautiful Pennant blue lacquer paint and tan vinyl upholstery to its engine, drivetrain, and every single piece of trim, hoses, clamps, and wiring, it's as if it just rolled off the St. Louis assembly line. Even the tires and exhaust system are original to this car. While it may be one of only 300 Corvettes built for the 1954 model year, today it's unquestionably the only one in existence that's been driven so few miles. If there's another, we would love to know about it.

Chapter 7

Authentic Europeans:
Unaltered Sports Cars and Sedans

It seems that European cars attracted car owners who were more concerned with compelling style, sophisticated engineering, and rewarding road-holding ability rather than brand loyalty. As a result, they usually took better care of their cars due to their great appreciation for them. Many were used strictly as weekend drivers or just summer transportation, thus there's an abundance of original European sports cars and sedans still wearing their original paint and interiors, and wearing them quite well.

In most cases, the more expensive the car, the more attention and greater care was lavished upon it. Mercedes-Benzs, it seems, were treated the best, as proven by the outstanding and incredibly well-preserved 1958 300 SL roadster and 1966 200D sedan that are featured on the following pages. Yet, as contrasted by another 1958 300 SL example that's well used proves, the high-end European cars can be both well cared for and driven with endless passion just as their makers engineered them to be.

At the other end of the spectrum, entry-level British sports cars when new were just that: cheap, fun transportation for those with limited budgets. Years of forgetful maintenance and aggressive, pleasure-seeking driving resulted in dings, dents, and worn interiors. So seeing such authentically preserved examples like the MGA Deluxe roadster and rubber-bumper MGB in this chapter is a real treat. The same applies to the featured early Porsche 911E, which is not only used regularly but driven on some of this country's most densely populated roads. And the Ferrari 275 GTB, with its original paint that looks as good as the day it was first applied, is not only an exceptional example of the breed but further cements this chapter's opening statement on European car owners.

Unlike American cars, European-built sports cars and sedans were shipped to the States in limited numbers, which is why it's a rare treat to happen upon an example that still retains all its original, fine European workmanship.

Discovering unrestored European cars that have remained in their original state isn't as common a sighting as happening upon original American family cars from the 1960s, but only because European cars weren't purchased as often. Be they low-end sports cars or high-end sedans, they are out there, so when you come across one, stop for a moment or two and give it a long inspection. Even though you may be a stubborn American-car enthusiast, you'll quickly appreciate everything that's unique about its distinctive build quality, workmanship of material, and nonconformist engineering and understand just why both the current and previous owners of it have been so protective and supportive of its originality.

A Big Apple Original

For more than three decades, this 1958 Mercedes-Benz 300 SL roadster has been driven throughout New York City and Long Island with great gusto.

SINCE THE DAY he purchased this 300 SL roadster, owner Steve Halpern of Hewlett Harbor, New York, has been using it as if it were a Ford Taurus. Whether he has to run down to the supermarket to buy milk or contend with the ever-crowded Southern State Parkway to get to Republic Airport in Farmingdale so he can work on his vintage 1946 Globe Swift airplane, he thinks nothing of hopping into his sleek classic Mercedes for the journey.

When I met Steve, he had just driven onto the show field at the Queens County Farm Museum in Floral Park, Queens, to take part in the New York Antique Automobile Club's annual April car show. Just as he's been doing for decades, he thought nothing of driving his preciously original 300 SL through the congested city streets and in the bumper-to-bumper traffic on the Cross

Island Parkway to get there. "I bought it to drive and enjoy," Steve said with a seemingly endless amount of enthusiasm for the car. "I love driving this car, and I plan on doing so until I can't drive anymore."

Of the 1,858 300 SL roadsters produced, just 324 were built for the 1958 model year. I can't help but think that, of all those in existence today, just how many have been restored or, at the very least, repainted. Not Steve's SL. Driven about 53,000 miles since new, it still wears its original, Mercedes-applied black paint and cream leather upholstery. Aside from a new clutch and pressure plate and the rebuilding of the mechanical fuel injection pump, no other mechanical work has ever been done, nor has it ever been needed. Most amazing is the fact that the brake linings, front and rear, have never needed changing.

Besides the Mercedes' originality and the way it drives and handles, what Steve likes most about it is its shape. He was quite adamant when he stated: "I love the convertible, and I still think it's the most beautiful car I've ever seen in my life."

The sheepskin seat covers have helped preserve the original leather upholstery; the Becker Mexico AM/FM radio was rebuilt by the German engineer who originally designed it. The car's original registration papers were attached to the steering column when the car was first sold, and have remained there, untouched, since 1958.

The 215-horsepower 2,996-cc straight-six overhead-cam engine has been free of mechanical maladies since day one. Apart from rebuilding the Bosch fuel injection pump and a thorough tune-up to get everything perfectly synchronized, the engine has provided flawless performance. From the dual ignition coils and associated wiring to the radiator, generator, and starter motors, every component is not only original but none have ever been removed since they were first bolted in place back in 1958.

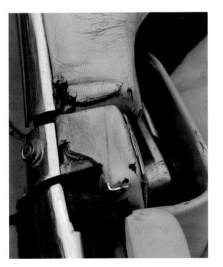

Steve fitted these vintage Suburban plates to his SL when he first registered the car back in 1975, and they have been there ever since. In several spots the reddish-brown primer below the original black paint is beginning to show through and part of the original leather is beginning to split in places, but there are no plans to fix either.

Matchless MG

An incredibly authentic 1962 MGA Deluxe that's still driven and enjoyed regularly.

WALKING INTO Carl Meyer's garage is like walking into an MG museum. There's a 1935 PB, 1939 TB, 1954 TF, 1960 MGA Twin-Cam, 1963 MGB, 1969 MGC-GT, 1973 MGB, a 1955 TF 1500 undergoing a body-off restoration in the back room, and our subject car, an unrestored 1962 MGA MK II Deluxe roadster. He also owns a 1953 Jaguar XK120 roadster and a 1968 Mercedes-Benz 280SL, but it's this well-preserved black MGA that is so dear to him.

Carl, a dentist from Slingerlands, New York, informed us that what he likes most about this original MG is, "its condition, and the fact that it has all its original tools, owner's manual, top, side curtains, etc. The interior is untouched, as are the seats and door panels, although there's some noticeable wear of the furflex door seals. The original vinyl on the scuttle is excellent and unique to the MK II. The car has period Amco floor mats, which protect the original black carpeting. In fact, its condition and rarity and its two-owner history prior to my purchase in 1994 are what make this particular MG so special."

When Carl first went to see the MG, it was exactly as you see it today, except the brakes were frozen. The car was stored in an upstate New York garage that had stone floors, but at least there was a plastic drop cloth on the ground below it that prevented the moisture in the ground from rising up and rotting the car's underside. "My original intention when I bought this MG was to enjoy it by driving it sparingly and preserve it in its original condition. I purchased the car with 13,011 miles on it. I also believe that this type of car has to be used to preserve its mechanical integrity. It was in a museum for one and a half years and I had to go back through it mechanically because it was not driven during that time."

Aside from this car's extraordinary original condition, including all its factory-applied exterior paint, chrome trim, and, most remarkably, the vinyl convertible top and side curtains (parts which rarely last long due to the fragile nature of their fabric and exposure to years of heat, cold, and rain) it's the limited-production rarity of this MGA that Carl also appreciates. He told us: "MG built 2,111 Twin-Cam models and had approximately 400 chassis left over after ending that model's production. These chassis, which sport front and rear disc brakes and the Twin Cam's distinguishing Dunlop knock-off solid wheels, were placed under MK I and MK II production bodies. The MK II is the last of the MGA series and uses the larger-displacement 1,622-cc four-cylinder pushrod engine, a new design that featured a stronger block, thus increasing torque and horsepower; this model also has the desirable close-ratio four-

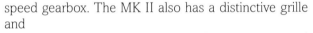

Still appearing like the day they were first screwed into place, it's rare to find original MGA door panels in this condition. More remarkable is the fact that both the convertible top and the side curtains are the very same pieces that were installed on the car at the MG factory.

speed gearbox. The MK II also has a distinctive grille and
taillamps. The last year of MGA production is 1962, and this car is one of just 290 MK II Deluxe roadsters produced."

Like most original cars, there are a few parts that have had to be replaced during its lifetime, and this incredibly original MGA is no exception. The fuel lines, spark plugs, points, and condenser are your typical wearing items and all were replaced, as were the exhaust system and brake pads. Apart from converting the electrical system to a single 12-volt battery, the brake master cylinder and wheel cylinders had to have their rubber internals replaced. "Maintaining the MG's originality is not that difficult," Carl said, "if you maintain it properly and store it properly. Routine maintenance and driving it periodically, as well as keeping it clean and waxed, simplify the task."

As to the continuing debate of restored versus original, Carl stated: "There just isn't any restoration (and I have done a few) that can duplicate this car's factory assembly and finish. It is tight and rattle free, door closure is tight and solid as if it just left the factory. Because of its condition, its driveability is superb. I'd say its driving character is what I like most." Carl went on to say that, "We are only caretakers, and I will keep this car as long as I possibly can. I would like to see it go to the British Motor Heritage museum in England. If not, then only to a die-hard collector of original cars."

Everything is original inside the trunk as well, including the spare tire cover, jack, tools, and air pump. Even the Michelin 5.90-15 tire is the very same spare that was placed in the trunk back in 1962.

The Derrington wood steering wheel is an authentic factory accessory that is highly sought after today, while the floor mats are period Amco mats. Aside from the Stewart-Warner amp gauge, all else is original to the car, even the carpeting, upholstery, and all the lift-the-dot fasteners.

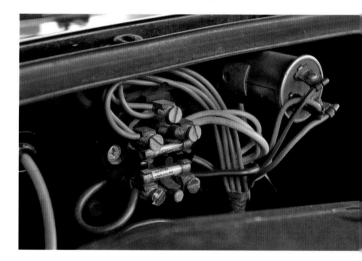

The valve cover was painted back in the early 1960s by the car's first owner, but all else has remained untouched. From the fabric-covered radiator hoses and their clamps to the black air ducting, which always seems to deteriorate, this MGA engine compartment is as original as you're ever likely to find.

Country-find Countryman

As authentic as Austin built it, estate sale finds like this 1965 Mini Countryman are still out there.

NO, THIS IS NOT AN abandoned Austin Mini. It's how cars look after they have been used sporadically then parked in a barn only to remain there for 12 years without any care or maintenance due to the death of its owner. Prior to that, it was the beloved sporting machine of its first owner, an American, who special-ordered the car while he was working in England and had it shipped to the States upon his return. During his ownership he kept it exactly the way it was built, mechanically, aesthetically, and otherwise.

Finding cars like this today may be getting more impossible as time marches on, but if you always keep your eyes open you just never know where one will turn up. Being a collector of anything old, Dave Brownell, Northeast representative for David Gooding Auctions and well-known old-car historian, happened to be reading his local newspaper when he spotted an ad for an estate sale, which listed this Mini among its offerings.

With no one else bidding on the car, Dave and his wife, Marian, ended up becoming the car's second owners. What they got was a 59,177-mile Mini Countryman, a model that was never officially imported into the United States. Although its green paint is dull, it's original to the car, as is its well-kept two-tone matching green vinyl interior.

The entire brake system, clutch and clutch master cylinder, and voltage regulator had to be replaced to make the Mini drivable, but that's all Dave plans on doing to the car at the moment. There are a few minor rust bubbles starting to show at the body seams that will one day have to be taken care of to prevent further rusting. Dave said, "Eventually it will need to be painted in order to prevent surface rust from spreading, which won't make it feel as original as it does now.

"This car's got personality, and it's in great condition. It's got the look, the feel, and the smell that it's meant to have. If it was restored it would be cute, but its personality would be different. Cars that have not been restored reflect the original intent of the designers, engineers, and builders. They are authentic. Besides, like this, we can use it as a daily driver."

From the green paint on its valve cover to the radiator, windshield washer bottle, and blower motor, everything has remained untouched since the Austin workers put them there in 1965. The oil cooler was installed early in the 848-cc engine's life, thus it looks original, too.

All the Smiths gauges, including the warning bulbs inside the 95-mile-per-hour speedometer, are in excellent condition, as well as the original toggle switches, the heater, and choke-pull knobs below. The exterior paint has dulled, but the emblems and trim remain shiny.

Apart from one small tear on the passenger-side front seat, the vinyl upholstery has held up extremely well, needing only a thorough cleaning to make it look new again. The matching vinyl door inserts are in equally excellent condition.

Stashed in the Barn

The quiet surroundings of Vermont's country-side provide a safe haven for this breathtaking collection of unrestored sports cars.

THAT OLD SAYING, "never judge a book by its cover," is easily applicable when talking about barns, especially the really rustic-looking ones here in Vermont. After discovering what was hidden away behind the worn wooden doors of this particular barn near where I live, I now tell everyone, "Never judge a barn by its wood."

For years I had passed by a sizeable barn with a stone wall in front and never gave a second thought to the contents on the other side of its weathered planks. I'd heard about a wonderful collection of some very desirable European sports cars that was nearby, but I never was able to find out where they were or who owned them. It wasn't until *Hemmings'* first concours, The New England Concours d'Elegance, which took place at Stratton Mountain in July 2007, that I finally met the man who put together this tantalizing collection of un-restored originals.

Because he values his privacy, I promised not to mention his name or the town in which his collection resides—for the sake of reference I will call him Mr. Vermont. But when I told him about this book project he was all too eager to have these rare gems photographed for your enjoyment.

With its radiant-heated concrete floor, the big barn houses six cars, four of which are well-preserved originals: a Jaguar XK120 coupe, Porsche 356 coupe, 1973 911 Carrera, and a 1971 BMW 2002 showing just 13,000 miles. The barn at the back of the property is where this stunningly original 1966 Ferrari 275 GTB is garaged along with an equally original 1958 Mercedes-Benz 300 SL roadster.

1966 Ferrari 275 GTB

If ever there's a marque that has seen way too many of its cars unnecessarily restored, it's Ferrari. For some reason, the majority of Ferrari owners think their cars must be restored to the highest level of concours perfection for them to compete with their peers. Now the tables have turned. With so few vintage Ferraris remaining in their original, unrestored state, these are the models that are fast becoming the most sought after to own. This Series III long-nose 275 GTB is perhaps one of the best.

"It's one of the most beautiful but menacing designs Ferrari ever produced. Great power, great sound," said Mr. Vermont of his prized prancing horse. In fact, he loves everything about this Ferrari, especially the stone chips on the nose, the slightly worn carpets, and the vintage racing decals on the windscreen from Elkhart Lake 1966.

With every square inch of its Rosso Corsa paint remaining just as it was applied back in Maranello, this is one of few GTBs in existence with 100 percent of its original body. Shortly after it was shipped to America, its original owner attended the June Sprints at Road America; the decals that he stuck to the windshield that day are still there.

When he purchased it at a Christie's auction at the Petersen Museum in Los Angeles in 2000, Mr. Vermont's goal was to "preserve it and get it in 100 percent driving condition, show it where appropriate in preservation events, and drive it enough to keep it sound. However, my biggest dilemma with owning such an incredible machine is not driving it enough," says Mr. Vermont. "It sits snowbound in a climate-controlled garage in Vermont six months a year."

With less than 14,000 miles on the odometer, Mr. Vermont said: "Original cars drive better, the doors close with the proper click, or thunk, and their rarity makes them so special. More important, it's a real honor to own what many people think is the most original GTB on the planet."

As shown by the odometer on its Veglia speedometer, just 13,974 miles have accumulated since day one. That's the reason why every aspect of this black leather interior is in exceptional as-made condition.

Still sporting its original Slate Gray metallic lacquer and leather interior, this 300 SL is considered by many experts to be one of the very best unrestored originals in existence. The canvas convertible top is also original, except for the patch that was placed there to cover a hole made by an anti-Mercedes mouse.

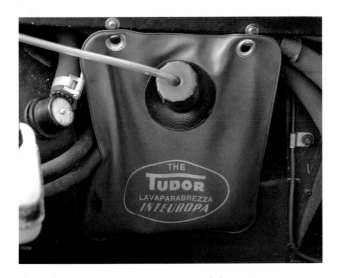

The 280-horsepower 3,286-cc V12 has never needed any major mainte-nance or repairs. Its six, two-barrel Webers, the black crackle finish on the cam covers, and the windshield washer fluid bag have never been apart, repainted, or replaced.

1958 Mercedes-Benz 300 SL Roadster

Unlike the well-used black 300 SL that is featured elsewhere in this book, this near identical 1958 model is the complete opposite. It's a low-mileage original that's been lovingly pampered its entire existence—it's been driven slightly less than 10,000 miles since new. The main aesthetic differences are the Rudge knock-off wheels, and because it's equipped with a high-performance camshaft its horsepower rating is 250.

"It's one of the most, perhaps *the* most, original 300 SL roadsters in the world," Mr. Vermont said about his cherished roadster. "The fit and finish are extraordinary. With its smooth-pulling engine it comes up on the cam nicely, thus making it a great driver. And with its Slate Gray metallic exterior and Terra Cotta red leather interior it has a terrific appearance. The color scheme is so subtle the car does not attract undue attention."

The biggest issue that Mr. Vermont has with this 300 SL is the paint. "I struggle with water spots on the original lacquer and just can't find a fix to the problem," he said. "And the foam inside the upholstered bolsters may be gradually disintegrating." Thankfully, that's all that is wrong with this beauty. At the 2003 Amelia Island Concours it garnered the Most Elegant Mercedes award, so perhaps that paint problem isn't such an issue after all.

"They are the real thing as the factory intended," Mr. Vermont said of original cars. "Not better than new, but 100 percent correct and authentic."

Unlike most 300 SL 2,996-cc straight-six engines that are rated at 215-horsepower, this powerplant is equipped with a special high-lift camshaft that allows it to develop a very healthy 250 horsepower.

It may look restored, but we can assure you that this interior is as original as they come. The VDO ammeter that's mounted below the dashboard in the center is a rare factory option, while the 9,749-mile odometer reading reached that mark during this photo shoot.

This 1973 Porsche 911RS blue-script Carrera is one of few all-original examples remaining. From its exterior white paint to its black sports seats to its high-revving flat-six 2.7-liter engine, complete with all factory-applied decals, it's a Porsche enthusiast's dream come true.

Although the darker gray color was applied back in the 1950s, everything else about this XK120 coupe has remained just as the crew at the Jaguar factory first made it. Its deep-red leather interior and wood dash are in fine condition with a pleasing patina that makes it inviting to be in. The 3,442-cc twin-cam-six has proven to be very reliable whenever called upon.

No European car collection is complete without a BMW 2002. This 1971 model has been driven just 13,000 miles. Its original-paint body is perfect, as are the shock towers, upholstery, door panels, and dashtop. An incredible unrestored specimen that every 02 fanatic will go crazy over.

Diesel Dream

Fastidious cleaning and regular use keeps this 1966 Mercedes-Benz 220D in fine form.

IT'S ALWAYS GOOD to let others know the type of cars you're interested in, because with any luck, they just may be acquainted with someone who has what you're looking for. The more you spread the word, the better your chances of making your automotive dreams come true.

Being connected to those in the collector-car industry is no doubt a huge help. This is how East Dorset, Vermont, resident Marian Savage, circulation director of *Auto Aficionado* magazine, and wife of noted automotive historian Dave Brownell, found the car she's spent years searching for. While we were hanging out in their barn among Dave's Morgan 4/4 and prewar Bentley, Marian told me "While talking to a colleague on the phone, I mentioned that I wished I could find a Mercedes-Benz 200D to replace the tired example I had years ago. That was in August 2005, and this is the car that came about as the result of that phone conversation.

"I had a 200D sedan years ago and loved it, but it wasn't in the condition that this one is in. I bought this four-door sedan from the car's second owner who knew everything about it. It came with lots of documentation, the factory manuals, and quite a few extra parts. The previous owner loved it so much he needed to be assured that it was going to a good home. He realized that

I was that person, who would appreciate it and provide a welcomed home for it."

What makes this 220D so unique is its red exterior. According to Marian, "The color is rare because this was a European Delivery car, and red was not available on U.S. models. The color is wonderful, and very unusual." Inspecting the body up close, I was amazed at the paint's overall quality. If you didn't know better you would think that this Mercedes was painted just a few months ago, its condition is that exceptional; even the underside of the hood and trunk lid, inside all four doorjambs and rain gutters look incredible, with nary a scratch or rust bubble in sight.

"To keep the paint looking its very best I have the car waxed twice yearly. Protecting its original red paint from oxidizing qualifies it for a place in our cramped garage, which means that my beloved, albeit slow, 1948 Willys Jeepster has to stay outside. The interior gets cleaned monthly or more if going to a show."

The black MB-tex vinyl upholstery, door panels, perforated headliner, dashboard, and multitone gray carpet are all original to this car and in excellent condition. The 1,988-cc four-cylinder 60-horsepower diesel engine with its Bosch mechanical fuel injection is all original too and works perfectly; only the brake system had to be rebuilt. Driven just 37,000 miles since new, this robust overhead-cam engine and its manual four-speed gearbox are barely broken in.

The Bosch mechanical injection has never needed any major servicing, nor did any other part of the 1,988-cc four-cylinder diesel engine. The firewall still sports the original vinyl-padded covering as well as all the other mechanical and electrical components that were installed at the factory.

While this well-preserved 200D is safely stored inside during Vermont's long, cold winter, when summer comes around Marian takes it out every chance she gets, but only if the weather is nice. "In the three years that we've owned it, I've been averaging a little more than 1,000 miles per year," Marian said. "Unlike restored cars, with originals you can enjoy them and use them without worrying about 'lowering their value.'"

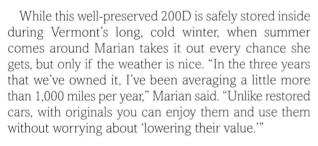

From the big white steering wheel and sliding heater controls to the square-weave carpet and MB-tex vinyl upholstery, as well as the black plastic sill covers, the entire cabin looks, feels, and even smells like a brand-new Mercedes.

Retaining that authentic sixties-era Mercedes cabin appeal, the original Becker Europa TR BC-FM radio is still in place and working perfectly. The finely crafted door panels, armrests, and handles are the recipient of fastidious care, and it shows.

Inside the well-preserved trunk resides the original screw jack, tools, and even the little plastic caps that cover the top of the shocks. All of the black paint is original to the car, and is still in very good condition.

Answering the Call

A want ad placed in Hemmings Motor News *is how this 1969 Porsche 911E was acquired.*

WHEN MY YOUNGER BROTHER David phoned me at work one day back in late 2006 saying that he wanted to replace the 1972 911 he had recently sold, I gave him some worthwhile older-brother advice: "Why don't you place a Wanted ad in *Hemmings Motor News*? You'll be surprised as to how many responses you'll get." This is how I found my Triumph TR3 and GT6, and a Vespa scooter for my youngest daughter. For once, David took my advice.

"I placed a 'Wanted: Father and Son Project' in the Porsche section and ended up buying this 911," David said. "About a half-dozen sellers called, and I ended up buying this particular example for three reasons. First: It was a 1969 E long-wheelbase B-series model. Second: It was the first series of fuel-injected 911s. Third: It was an original, rust-free Texas car that had only two owners.

"The car was an unrestored original that needed only minor work. It had not been running for two years, the fuel-injection belt had broken, front brake calipers froze, and the gas had gone bad. But it had all the original factory manuals, tools and jack, and its two previous owners retained all documentation including dealer maintenance records from day one."

Having owned about eight 911s before buying this car, David was seeking an honest, solid example, the kind of car that you never want to part with. "I finally got a 'keeper,'" he proudly said. "It's original, rust free, and a great driver. Knowing that it was well maintained and unmolested, it still has many thousands of miles of driving pleasure left before I take a second mortgage on my house attempting to rebuild it. Es are special in that they were the first fuel-injected 911s like the S but with a milder cam that affords them better drivability. And the Irish Green exterior color appealed to me because you see too many white, black, and red Porsches."

When I drove this 911 for a way-too-brief drive, I was amazed as to how solid it felt compared to David's other 911s, and how responsive the steering, acceleration, and brakes were for a car that was nearly 40 years old. Upon closer inspection, I noticed that one of the rear quarter panels had been repainted sometime in the past, but there was no sign of an accident; perhaps a minor fender scrape. The rest of the paint was well preserved. So, too, were all of the car's usual wearing items. According to David, "All gauges are original and in working order along with the dash, cabin, and driving lamps. The dash pad is badly cracked beyond repair in several areas due to that hot Texas sun over the last 38 years."

As one would expect from a car this age, not every part is original. The factory-equipped Boge self-leveling

Swedish Endurance

Holding up well to Volvo's famed quality of construction, if ever the world's most perfect 1973 144E exists, this is it.

"BASIC, EVERYDAY TRANSPORTATION." That's all that Carlos Heiligmann of Rowe, Massachusetts, wanted when he walked into the Jack Pickard Dodge-Volvo dealership in Greensboro, North Carolina, on July 13, 1973, while on a trip to visit his family. "It was my first car after graduating from college," Carlos proudly remembers. "I wanted a practical, safe, sturdy, and reliable car that would last a long time."

The cost for this standard-equipped 144E with the B20F four-cylinder 112-horsepower engine and M-40 four-speed manual gearbox was $4,465. There's not a single option on the car. The Hella headlamps and Cibie fog lamps were installed by Carlos, as was the Becker AM/FM radio.

Thanks to Carlos' fastidious care and demanding maintenance program, this one-owner Volvo just very well may be the best all-original 144E in the world. Upon close inspection, the factory-applied dark green paint is perfect, without a single noticeable chip or scratch. And it shines just as brightly as the day it was painted back at the Volvo factory in Sweden. All the exterior trim and chrome is perfect, too, especially the seats, which have been covered since Carlos first bought the car to pro-

tect the medium brown cloth fabric from getting dirty and worn. And every square inch of the dashboard is flawless as well, ditto for the door panels, carpeting, headliner, glass, weather stripping, and every single component in the engine compartment. Although the car looks as if it's been restored to a very high standard, it hasn't. Simply put, this is the absolutely best original car I have ever encountered.

Although the odometer reads 74,747 miles, one of the reasons this Volvo has remained in such incredibly original condition is because it's only driven from April to October. Avoiding New England's harsh winters is a good thing if you want your cars to remain in fine shape, which is something that Carlos has managed to do quite well. So just before winter sets in, the Volvo goes back into the garage and his 1978 Pontiac station wagon becomes the family workhorse; driven 264,000 miles to date, this too is a well-kept original.

When asked about the difficulty of maintaining the Volvo's originality, Carlos said, "It has provided many challenges in keeping it running. The combination of point-type ignition with Bosch D-jetronic fuel injection creates a unique set of trouble-shooting opportunities. Eventually, I installed an electronic ignition. Unfortunately, parts are quite expensive. I recently priced a new fuel pump and it was over $300. And the original dark green paint requires special care. But the car is sturdy and very comfortable for long trips."

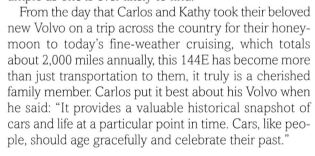

Since the first week of ownership, the front and rear seats were covered with custom-fitted seat covers; the original Volvo cloth material underneath is in absolute factory-mint condition. So too are the door panels, carpets, headliner, and everything else throughout the pristine, perfect interior.

Carlos was really telling the truth when he said, "In this 'throw-away' culture, it's nice to own and cherish an original." Truer words could never have been spoken, especially from Carlos, and that's because this Volvo isn't his only unrestored, all-original collector car. Elsewhere in this book is Carlos' 1947 De Soto. And stored in his basement, among his vintage Lionel train collection and expansive layout, there's his and his wife, Kathy's, 1978 Mercedes 230 sedan and Kathy's 1976 MGB; both cars look like they rolled off the assembly line just yesterday. Each car as perfect an original example as one is ever likely to find.

From the day that Carlos and Kathy took their beloved new Volvo on a trip across the country for their honeymoon to today's fine-weather cruising, which totals about 2,000 miles annually, this 144E has become more than just transportation to them, it truly is a cherished family member. Carlos put it best about his Volvo when he said: "It provides a valuable historical snapshot of cars and life at a particular point in time. Cars, like people, should age gracefully and celebrate their past."

As unbelievable as it may seem, the entire engine compartment is an untouched original. It has always been fastidiously maintained, ensuring that dirt never accumulated anywhere. From the paint on the firewall and shock towers to the weather stripping, wiring, decals, hoses, and clamps, everything has been perfectly preserved.

Every square inch of the factory-applied green enamel shines like the day it was first applied. Even the doorjambs, which still wear the original safety decals and whose hardware still shows its original anodized finish, look like they have just been restored.

Both the brake power booster and its factory white paint marking still appear brand new; so too do the three underhood insulation panels. Even the plastic on the chrome handbrake and the adjoining sill plate have remained scuff-free after all these years.

Authentically Abingdon

Caringly protected since new, this finely preserved 1980 MGB still runs and drives exceptionally well.

REMEMBER ALL THOSE rust-protection companies that were popular back in the 1960s and 1970s? With names like Ziebart, Ming, and Rusty Jones, how could anyone forget? Thankfully, many car owners saw fit to invest the hundred or so dollars that it cost for these shops to rustproof their beloved cars, the result of which is the absolute cause for these cars surviving today, with their unprotected counterparts falling victim to the dreaded tin worm.

One such car that benefited greatly from the Rusty Jones treatment is this incredibly solid and, of course, rust-free 1980 MGB. "It's original condition, low mileage, and it was rust-free due to rustproofing when new," are the main reasons owner Mark McCourt, an associate editor at *Hemmings Motor News*, gave when asked about his reasoning for buying this particular MGB. "With only 47,000 showing on the odometer, obviously it was a well-cared-for and beloved car."

Mark's father, Dennis, found the car advertised in his local newspaper. It was being sold by its second owner, who lived in Saugerties, New York. In fact, before Mark bought it from his dad and took it to Vermont, it had spent its entire life in the Hudson Valley region, which is just up the Hudson River from New York City.

"I always joke that this is the car that 'missed' British Leyland's quality control, because of its almost unfailing reliability," Mark proudly stated. "I've resisted the urge to modify it for increased performance and comfort. Original cars still have their factory-installed soul, spirit—the essence of Abingdon, the spirit of generations of MGs, and the hardy enthusiasts who drove them. Once they're taken apart, stripped, and repainted, they lose that soul. They may be pretty again, but their magic is gone."

Mark went on to say, "The interior is nearly all factory original. Mice have eaten two holes in the driver's seatback. The jute backing of the battery cover carpeting is disintegrating, so I have to vacuum carefully. The period rubber floor mats have protected the floor carpets well. The driver's door pull is starting to fail, and the rubber seals at the A-posts have dry-rotted and need replacement."

The only improvements that Mark plans on doing is to rebuild the suspension with stock components and make sure the braking system is up to snuff, which is important when the car is being used several times a week. Although the car's only been driven 58,867 miles since new, today it only averages about 500 miles per year.

"I could never imagine giving this car up—it's been a big part of my car-enthusiast life, and will always be."

As a result of the car's considerate owners, some of the MGB's hard-to-find original parts are still with this well-preserved roadster, including the tonneau cover, spare tire jack and its vinyl storage bag, owner's manual, 1980-specific speedometer, and decals. Tough-wearing factory vinyl has withstood the test of time very well.

Every square inch of the MGB's body shell remains covered in the same Porcelain White enamel that the British Leyland painters sprayed on the car when it was first built nearly 30 years ago.

The 1,800-cc overhead-valve four-cylinder engine has never been apart and starts right up every time thanks to a Weber carb conversion; the original Solex carb has been put aside for safekeeping. All instructional decals are original to the car.

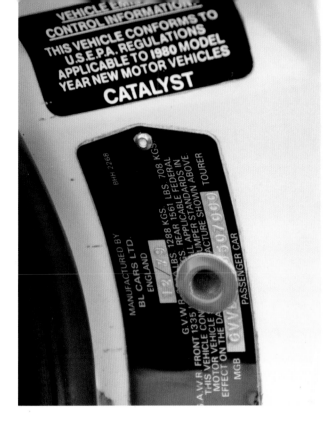

The red plastic plug is the aftermath of the rust-proofing material injected into the lower B-pillar—the result is a body that has remained completely free of rust.

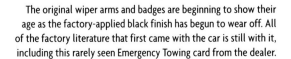
The original wiper arms and badges are beginning to show their age as the factory-applied black finish has begun to wear off. All of the factory literature that first came with the car is still with it, including this rarely seen Emergency Towing card from the dealer.

Chapter 8

Future Classics: Buy Them Now, While You Can

Now's the time to buy the cars that enthusiasts and collectors will be clamoring for 20 years from now. Just because you missed out on buying unrestored 1950s-era convertibles and 1960s muscle cars at the right price, that doesn't mean that you still can't put together a sizeable collection of original collector cars today. Looking into the future, there's a whole bunch of noteworthy late-model cars from the 1980s and 1990s that will soon become highly sought after by collectors and enthusiasts in the know. Not only is the time right to buy, but your chances of finding one that's an unre-painted original will never be better.

The car that heads the top of the list is the 1979–1993 Fox-bodied Mustangs. Because the majority of them were raced, modified, and customized, owning a bone-stock original, especially the 1987–1993 models, will pay off in the long run. The other top-tier cars to own include Buick's GNX and GNs, third- and fourth-generation Camaros and Firebirds, Monte Carlo SSs, Hurst/Olds, Taurus SHOs, and fourth-generation Corvettes, especially unmolested ZR-1s. LT1-powered Buick Road-master station wagons will soon be in great demand as will Chevy's Impala SS.

Regarding imports, low-mileage first-generation Miatas and the last of the old-style Mercedes SL roadsters will be highly coveted, as will early-style Audi TTs and BMW M3s, any Porsche 911, and even the early Volkswagen GTi.

Today's enthusiasts cars are tomorrow's collectibles. Chevrolet's Impala SS is one such example out of many late-model cars that can still be easily found in original, factory-built condition.

Truth be told, any well-maintained original car that sports its original paint and interior will be desirable to own, especially any and all full-size station wagons and performance-oriented pickup trucks. I can even see the day when an authentic first-generation Chrysler minivan turns heads at Hershey. Those days will soon be here, so buy now. All of these cars, and more, are as close as your nearest newsstand.

Sharp Friends

*The remarkable originality of these
Hurst/Olds brought together the owners
who fast became close friends.*

MORE OFTEN THAN NOT, if a car has been produced in limited numbers, chances are much greater it will be better cared for and driven sparingly throughout its life. Such is the case with both of these Hurst/Olds—the black and silver car is a 1983 model, while the silver and black car is a 1984.

Both cars are regulars at the summer cruise-ins that take place in the parking lot of *Hemmings Motor News.* As a result of their incredible originality and well-maintained nature, both were featured in *Hemmings Muscle Machines* magazine, issue #2, November 2003.

1983 Hurst/Olds Cutlass

Oldsmobile built just 3,001 Hurst editions for the 1983 model year; this black beauty is car number 2664. "My brother-in-law bought it from Action Chevrolet in Troy, New York, in 1985," said owner Paul Maxon, also of Troy. "It was so well cared for, it had covers on the front seats for as long as I've known the car, and the upholstery has probably never been touched. No worn or faded spots, and not a single rip or tear."

With some 36,500 miles on the car, as expected, the tires had to be replaced; however, Paul has the original tires stored in his garage. Besides the battery, the intake manifold gasket and the front universal joint had to be replaced, too. But that's all. The factory-applied paint is just as perfect as a new car. Paul makes sure that the body is clean at all times and keeps the finish protected with regular applications of Meguires wax. ArmorAll is applied to all interior surfaces several times a year.

Although the body panels and all of its mechanical components are virtually the same as all the other hundreds of thousands of Cutlasses that Oldsmobile produced during this era, certain body parts that are specific to the Hurst models are getting very hard to find. The rear wing, front air dam, the dual air breather on the carburetor, and, of course, the lightning rod shifters because they were used only on the 1983–1984 cars.

Yet, regardless of the difficulty in owning a car whose parts are irreplaceable and maintaining its integrity is a never-ending battle, Paul was steadfast in his position on the value of originality versus restoration. "The best thing about unrestored cars, such as this Hurst/Olds, is that if you ever decide to sell them, people would know exactly what they are buying.

"Wherever I take it, it always gets a lot of attention; most people have no conception of how rare these cars are. Because of their rarity, my goal is to maintain its originality as best I can."

With no reproduction upholstery available, it's a good thing that the original Maple Red velour cloth fabric is in perfect condition. So, too, is the maroon-colored steering wheel and dashboard. Lightning rod shifters still function in a most accurate manner.

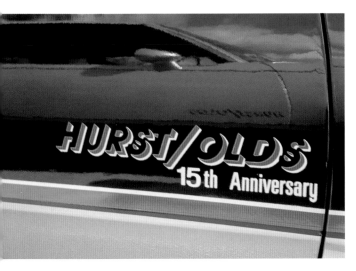

The 1983-model car wore these special badges celebrating the 15th Anniversary of Oldsmobile's collaboration with Hurst. Each one of these special badges, including the 15th Anniversary decal on the driver's side door, is unspoiled.

1984 Hurst/Olds Cutlass

When I tried to contact owner Steve Gallant, whom I had known since 2003 when I photographed his car for *Hemmings Muscle Machines*, about featuring his silver Hurst/Olds in this book, I sadly learned that he had unexpectedly passed away shortly before Christmas, 2007. Thankfully, Steve's son, Chris, who now owns the car, agreed to have this Olds featured in memory of his father.

Both Hurst/Olds have led similar lives, and both are in excellent original condition. This silver example now shows 47,000 miles on its odometer, has had basically none of its parts replaced, and was owned by just one previous owner, too.

Chris, who resides in West Sand Lake, New York, said: "My father purchased it in the spring of 1998 because when he first saw this car he felt it was a rare find worth grabbing. I believe my father's intention was to enjoy driving the car while maintaining its beauty. He was a car enthusiast and enjoyed taking it to various car shows. Continuing in his footsteps is a great honor for me. This car is one of the ways I have of remembering my dad and all of the good times and enjoyment it brought him. Being able to further its existence in the way he would have is sort of my own personal tribute to him. The only thing I intend to do is keep doing what my father did—after all, this was my father's Oldsmobile."

Like Steve, Chris also prefers cars that are original. "Unrestored cars are in the purest form since their creation," said Chris. "While restoring a vehicle takes considerable amounts of time and money, you only have one chance at keeping a car original. The fact that this car hasn't been tampered with is what gives the car its character. Even the radio has never been replaced. As the years go by, to see a car in its purest stock form is really something."

Thankfully, Chris isn't planning any modifications to this desirable GM G-body.

"Since I just acquired it, I'm not too sure what to expect, but I imagine the hardest thing will be preserving all of the rare and next-to-impossible-to-replace items that define the car."

While it's no torque monster, the 180-horsepower, 307-ci V8 on both cars provides a sufficient amount of get up. The four-barrel Quadra-Jet carb, four-speed TH 200-4R, and every single inch of vacuum hose and hardware have remained just as Oldsmobile built them.

The impossible-to-replace waterfall grille, which is different from the egg-crate grille of the 1983 model, has remained crack-free; all the original badges, lenses, and trim, both inside and out, are in equally perfect condition.

The factory-applied plastic coating on the five-spoke 15x7-inch Hurst Super Sport wheels has protected the chrome and Argent Silver paint and the outer rim's red stripe well.

High-Mileage Collectible

Just because it's been driven 170,000 miles doesn't mean that this 1996 Chevrolet Impala SS isn't a well-preserved original.

"IT'S THE LAST OF A BREED. The last full-size, full-frame, rear-drive GM passenger car," said Terry McGean, executive editor of *Hemmings Motor News* of his prized 1996 Impala SS. "It's an unmodified example of the best and last year Chevy offered the Impala, which is why I wanted this particular example."

A General Motors enthusiast, Terry knows a thing or two about Chevys. His summer daily driver is a 1967 Camaro, and he has owned a 1969 Camaro since the mid-1980s. Realizing that the Impala SS will one day soon become a sought-after collector car, and the fact that an original one will be far more desirable than one that's been modified, he looked long and hard and finally found this rare Dark Gray-Green metallic example. It's a car that was kept in fantastic condition by its original owner, whose family sold it to Terry after their father passed away.

"What I appreciate most about original cars, regardless if they are 1960s-era vintage or late-model fuel-injected cars from the 1990s, is the fact that I like having an example that seems the way the factory intended it to be," Terry said. "Plus, nobody messed around with it; it's all GM, no aftermarket junk. Its well-preserved

condition makes it seem very factory fresh. And the amount of miles on it don't bother me—these cars last a long time with proper care."

Even though it's been driven 170,000 miles, the fact that this SS has been meticulously maintained means that the chances are great that its paint, interior, engine, and mechanicals will remain in top-notch original condition. Terry's recipe to sustain its GM-built originality for years to come is quite simple. His advice: "Periodic detailing of the paint with a good-quality wax such as Mothers or Meguires, always garage it in winter, and never drive in snow or on salt-covered roads. In the summer I shade the interior from sun when parked outside, and regularly treat the leather with pro-grade leather-care products."

The best thing about collecting late-model cars like the Impala SS is that you still have the opportunity to buy original-equipment spare body and trim parts, and for reasonable prices, which is virtually impossible for older cars. That is why Terry scours swap meets and Internet sites, seeking any new SS parts he can find, particularly spares such as emblems and interior wear items.

Like all the other car owners whose cars are profiled in this book, Terry feels the same as they do about the advantages of owning a car that has never been restored: "A car is only original once; that can't be reclaimed once it's gone. Even great restorations that have

better fit and finish than new often don't function as new—doors don't close right, windows don't operate smoothly, finishes and fasteners are wrong or too nice. An original car looks, works, drives, and maybe even smells like it did when new, or at least the way you might remember it from years ago. Restorations usually don't capture that. Plus, it's easier to keep a good car nice than to try to return it to nice after it gets beat up, worn out, and otherwise abused."

Driving across the United States, the big Impala proved to be an excellent highway cruiser, returning 26 miles per gallon on average, and that was at a steady 75–80 miles per hour.

Fitted with the 1996-only analog gauge cluster and soft leather upholstery, this is the most desirable late-model Impala SS to own. You can still buy them with interiors as nice as this.

The floor-shifter was another welcomed change that was only fitted to the 1996 models. Finding consoles in this fine condition and all four five-spoke wheels without curb rash is quite unusual.

Index